Ghostly Tales of Minnesota

by Ruth D. Hein

Adventure Publications
Cambridge, Minnesota

Edited by Hazel Retzlaff
Cover design by Jonathan Norberg
Book design by Patricia Wagner

15 14 13 12
Copyright 1992 by Ruth D. Hein
Published by Adventure Publications, Inc.
820 Cleveland Street South
Cambridge, MN 55008
1-800-678-7006
www.adventurepublications.net

ISBN: 978-0-934860-79-6

Acknowledgements

In the preface to *Ghostly Tales of Southwest Minnesota* (1989), I admitted that there were "more ghosts lurking in this area" than I could fit into that book. I didn't know then that I would be the one to record them before they are forgotten or that I would find ghost stories from other parts of the state.

But this new collection, *Ghostly Tales of Minnesota*, would not have materialized without the help of the storygivers. I needed to know about their experiences so that I could build my stories around them.

My sincere thanks to all who either told me a story or told me where to find one. Special thanks to correspondent Diana Anderson, who let me use her story that appeared in the Worthington *Daily Globe*'s Halloween issue as the core of my story "Serenity Disrupted." And many thanks to the publisher and editors who helped to perfect this book.

With the help of library and historical society materials and personnel, historians and newspapers, I was able to research settings and backgrounds. Some names and locations are disguised to respect the wishes of the storygivers.

Finally, thanks to my husband and family for not putting me on trial for being, once again, so "preoccupied with ghosts."

Dedication

This book is dedicated to...

The Ghosts

without whom
this collection of stories
would not be possible.

Table of Contents

A Hovering, Smothering Spirit

Grandma Emma was glad that the day had come to an end. Tidying up had taken a while. The grandchildren had hauled out all the toys as they thought of them. Bingo and Checkers had to be put back on the shelf; Slap and Crazy Eights and the other card games had to be put back in their basket.

Usually that was done before they left. They were good about that. But this time was different. There was the call saying the sheep were out on the road and everyone, including Grandpa Will, left in a hurry. Emma had everything straightened up by the time Will came home. "Well, that should be the last time now. We fixed the fence while we were at it," he said.

"Did they just push it down, or what happened, Will?

"They got to rubbing their backs and necks on the barbed wire. You know how they do. You can tell by the wool caught in the wire. That strained the stakes until they tipped, and the sheep just walked the fence down and got out. But we took care of it."

"Good. I'm tired. I'll bet you are, too. I think I'll just call it a day and crawl in."

"See you later, then," Will said. "I'm gonna watch the news and weather first."

And so Emma crawled in, pulled the covers up, and settled in for sleep.

Their home was on a farm on the edge of a town not far from Worthington. They weren't farming the land anymore. They said they had retired. It was a quiet place, and sleep came soon enough that night. But it didn't last long. Emma began to struggle and hit out toward something - she didn't know what it was - but she felt as though she was being smothered. Her actions woke her. She looked around the room. Nothing there. She felt foolish as she realized she must have been dreaming.

Another night, about a week later, Emma again struggled in her sleep. This time the feeling was the same, but she also saw a gray, indefinite mass coming down toward her. "Will! Will!" she cried out. Will snapped awake and turned on the lamp. He looked at his wife there beside him. She was all right, but she looked and sounded all washed out when she told him she must have had a nightmare.

This went on for a long time. It didn't happen every night, but off and on. At first, Will tried to tell Em she was just tired out and sleeping poorly and having dreams. But Emma wasn't convinced. The more she thought about it and tried to relive the feeling or the happening or to tell someone else about it, the more it troubled her. Each time it happened, it was as though a gray mass came down to smother her. When it seemed to bear down upon her shoulders and neck, as if closing in on her, she'd wake up and scream. Will always quieted her and comforted her. He put his arm over her and told her, "It was just another dream. Try an' get back to sleep."

That only helped temporarily, and after many restless nights for both of them, Will told a neighbor down the road about the dreams. Henry listened carefully and spoke up after Will finished. "Now Will, Em might just be having dreams. But on the other hand, there may be something more to it."

"What d'ya mean, Henry?"

"Why, they might not be dreams at all. Do you believe in spirits?"

"Ya mean, like good spirits an' evil spirits, an' stuff like that?"

"Yah - or the spirit of someone that died and is still hanging around."

"Still hanging around! What on earth...! There's no one rattling around in that old house but the two of us and I don't want to hear nothin' more 'bout spirits!"

"But, Will, didn't you know that there was a murder in the house you bought? It happened a long time ago. Most of the neighbors just got used to knowing it and sort of forgot about it, I guess. Matter of fact, so did I - until you told me about Em's dreams, or whatever."

"You might as well tell me the rest of the story now. Even if I might not be able to sleep because of it!"

"All I know is that someone was murdered in that house, long ago. Come to think about it, it seems to me it was a woman. Say, what room are you two sleeping in?"

"We took the one on the second floor, back in the northwest corner."

"Why, I believe that's the room where the murder happened. But that's all I do know about it. And I gotta get for home now. Sorry I had to be the one to tell you."

"Henry, thanks for telling me. It makes more sense now. If the spirit of that person is hovering in her old room, maybe she's upset. We just have to do something about it. We have to confront it, I guess."

The next time the dream or the hovering gray mass or the gray ghost or whatever it was appeared to be closing in on Emma, Will spoke up. He emphatically announced to everyone present, meaning him and Em and the ghost, that there was no need to be upset or jealous or angry or anything else. That Emma had nothing whatsoever to do with the murder. That she didn't even know it had taken place. "And now, be so kind as to leave us in peace!" were his final words that night.

Though the spirit never appeared again, Emma still had a hard time getting to sleep some nights. She couldn't help remembering those troubled, sleepless times. She couldn't help but wonder if it was a dream, or a presence, or if it was connected with that murder Will had told her about. But once she knew about that, she could understand the strange appearances, though they ceased abruptly the night Will spoke out.

Will and Emma moved into Worthington a few years later. The house and the farm buildings on the old place were destroyed as a matter of course. And though she still wonders what the deal was, Emma sleeps soundly in her new home and surroundings. "Somehow, I feel lighter, as if a weight had been lifted from me. Maybe it was. I'll always wonder."

The Old Arch Thom Place

Time brings change. As generations pass, old buildings are destroyed, new ones built; old trees are cut down, young ones planted; people move out, others move in. With all the changes that took place on one farm west of Rushmore, one would have to know the site if one wanted to find it now. The buildings are gone. The huge barn, still there in 1978 is gone. The house was finally burned down by a descendant tired of the constant need for repairs or replacements.

The beautiful apple orchard that grew near the house is gone; there is no grove of tall cottonwoods north of the barn. Even the stumps have been grubbed out for a couple more acres of tillable land. There was a cistern under the floor of the house; since there is no house, there is no floor, though the cistern casing may still be there, well below the surface.

All that's left is a couple lines of shrubby trees, planted later, that border the old house yard. All the land beyond those trees is farmed. Once the requirements of the tree-planting program that provided the seedlings are met, farm machinery will probably move right through the only untilled space, the yard. Then there will be no visible sign, but the stories will not be as easily wiped out.

Folks talk about "the old Arch Thom place." Because of some strange things that happened there long ago, people refer to it as "the Arch Thom haunted house," even with the house gone. Several members of the Thom family were unable to recall any ghostly incidents from the years the Thom family lived there, yet threads of stories indicate there must have been something to it.

After Arch Thom left the farm, they say he operated the Rushmore Elevator. He rented out the house and farm for a while around 1915, to John and Grace De Yonge and their thirteen children. The children who remember the incidents best are their son George De Yonge of Pierre, South Dakota and his sister Angeline Klaahsen of Sibley, Iowa. When they think back to those early years, they remember odd events.

Angeline recalls something happening on the stairway to second floor. She said, "Sometimes when we went down, it felt like someone was giving us a gentle push forward. There was a door at the bottom of the stairs, and then the dining room was next. Once Dena fell at the bottom of the steps. Mother asked, 'What's the matter with you?' and Dena said, 'It was like I was tripped, and all of a sudden I was on the dining room floor.' Other times she said, 'I got pushed!' It happened every now and then. The door would burst open and we'd look, and there was Dena, on her knees beyond the bottom step."

It wasn't usually hard for Angeline's mother Grace to keep track of the young ones playing together; she usually knew where they were by listening for them. One day, they were all outside near the plum trees while Grace worked in the kitchen. When she heard children playing and talking upstairs, she went up to see what they were doing inside, but she couldn't find anyone up there. They were all out in the yard, just as she had thought.

Of course, the children heard bits of their elders' conversations. When Grace and John talked of these mysterious incidents, the children became aware that there was something different about their house, and they wondered.

Grace seemed to be most aware of the strange feeling, especially in the south bedroom intended to be the master bedroom. They used it only for storage while they lived there. Grace was always reluctant to use it as a bedroom. When she was in that room, she was sometimes heard saying, "That's enough of this nonsense," or "You can leave here any time now." When the children heard her, they wondered.

George remembers one night when he was going out to the barn. "It was real dark out," he says. "We didn't have yard lights like now. And I didn't take a lantern along, 'cause I figured I knew the way well enough. I was on the path to the barn, but closer to our blacksmith shop that stood between the house and the barn. When I heard strange noises coming from the shop, I turned around and headed back to the house. I reached it in nothin' flat. Never did remember what I was gonna do in the barn that night."

Around 1915, it was not surprising when folks lost their way and had to stop somewhere for directions or a place to stay the night. "One pretty young school teacher driving her pony-drawn buggy got lost on a moonless night. She couldn't see the turns in the road, but somehow she found our house," George said. "Maybe she saw the mailbox out by the road and turned up the lane. Anyway, she was so bewildered that she was nearly hysterical when she knocked on the kitchen door.

"Mother lit a kerosene lamp and led her to a room where she could rest until morning. I put her pony up in the barn, with feed and water. At daylight, the poor woman looked like she hadn't slept for a month. Mother sent her in the right direction for wherever she had to go, and we never saw her again. But we always wondered if she was so shaken up because she was lost, or if something out there had scared her."

Grace's husband John used to tell their children one of the stories that hasn't died out. John said, "One night that same year, when we lived in that old farmhouse near Rushmore, someone banged hard on our door. It was real dark outside and in the house, too, because it was bedtime and we'd already put the lamps out. When I lit a lamp and opened the door, the man standing there said, 'I'm lost, and it's so dark out here I can't see my hands in front of my face.'

"I asked him in. He said he farmed down near Bigelow, but he didn't want to spend the rest of the night trying to find his farm. He said, 'I could see just enough out there to see the outline of your big, white house. I'm sorry I got you out of bed, but I didn't know what else to do.'

"We didn't talk any more after I showed him where he could sleep. The next morning, he was up bright and early and ready to go on his way. 'Gotta make up for lost time,' he said, 'and get for home now. By the way, what place is this?' Father says he answered, 'Why, this is the Arch Thom place, and we're the De Yonges.'

"When the fellow heard that, he said, 'Man - if I'd known this was the Arch Thom place, I wouldn't have stopped here for a thousand dollars. You could have shot me dead 'fore I'd a stayed here!' and out the door he went without so much as a thank you."

At least these few threads have now been put down for generations who will read the story but not be able to find any signs of the old house.

That is, unless the ghost responsible for these incidents and others, like those the lost farmer must have heard about, returns to show them the way.

Boomer's Bristling at Something

Some years ago, Eleanor and Rosie were sorting books in an upstairs bedroom of Eleanor's two-story house in Tracy. Eleanor and Clarence's dog Boomer was with them as usual, though he was no help at all with the books. Rosie told the story later.

"When Boomer started to growl," Rosie said, "I looked up and I could see the hair on his back raise up. I mentioned it to Eleanor and she said someone was probably out in the yard or going by the house. I wasn't so sure.

"Eleanor said, 'Why, Rosie, do you think there's someone hiding in the closet or something?'

"Eleanor checked out the closet, poking into every corner and reaching between the hanging clothes. She found nothing that didn't belong there.

"We went back to sorting the books. Boomer went back to growling and making a fuss. He was so restless! We got to feeling like something wasn't right, and it scared us.

"We followed each other closely down the hall and downstairs to the kitchen. Boomer followed us down, and we closed the stairway door.

"But he didn't let us relax over our coffee. He kept going back over to the stairway door and growling, his hair raised again.

"Clarence was at work, but when El called to tell him how the dog was acting and how frightened we were, he came home to check it out. He tried to get Boomer to come upstairs with him, but the dog wouldn't follow him. He'd go about halfway up, and then he'd stop and growl, staring ahead up the stairway.

"Clarence finally gave up on Boomer and checked the closet and the whole upstairs himself.

"We never did find anyone hiding up there that day, or anywhere else in the house. But we thought Boomer must have sensed something or someone unfamiliar. We tried to tell ourselves that maybe Boomer got scared of a little mouse that we couldn't see.

"Eleanor and I began to tell others in the neighborhood about it.

"They listened and sort of clammed up.

"Later on, El and I went to visit John, one of her elderly neighbors who had lived across the street. During the conversation, John asked El if they still had their dog. He laughed when he remembered the name they had given him, because the dog really didn't make much noise at all; he growled and bristled more than he barked.

"That reminded us of the day Boomer growled and bristled at nothing - at least, nothing we could see. We told John about it.

"John thought for a minute before he said, 'Well, there might have been something there, if you believe in spirits. There was a time, Eleanor, in the first years that I lived across from your house, that a man hanged himself there. I believe he was found upstairs, in that same bedroom, in the closet. Isn't that the one where you can slide the ceiling panel over to get up into the attic?'

"John was quiet a while. Then he continued, 'They say he fastened the rope to a ring in the attic rafters and then went back down the ladder, leaving the attic access panel open. When he was ready, he kicked the chair out from under himself, out into the bedroom.'"

Doorknobs, Dishes, and Disappearing Acts

Jacques "Jack" Tolsma is a businessman in Worthington. People who know him and his family also know about things that happened on his grandfather's farm not many miles from the Minnesota/Iowa border. In the mid-thirties, when Jack was seven or eight, he lived in the small, two-story home on that farm with his father, mother, sister, and Uncle Sy.

"Dad and Mother had the downstairs bedroom," Jack said, "and the rest of us slept upstairs. My room was the small northwest bedroom. A crazy thing that happened there has stuck with me all these years. At night, I'd shut the door when I went to bed. Before long, I'd hear the knob turn. The door would open about a foot. I'd get up, close it, and get scared. It happened enough times that I told the others about it.

"Uncle Sy tried to help me figure it out. He slept in my room, too, for a while and it happened again. Uncle Sy would get up and shut the door, and shut it good, and it would open again about a foot...never all the way. Whenever we blew out the kerosene lamp, we would hear the doorknob turn. Then the door would open, and Uncle Sy would get up and close it. Sometimes at night I think I'm still hearing the sound of that knob turning.

"We started putting a skeleton key in the keyhole and locking the door from inside the room, leaving the skeleton key in place. As soon as we blew out the lamp, we'd hear the sound of a key turning, then falling to the floor. When we got up to look, the skeleton key would be on the floor.

When Sy lit the lamp again, the door would be open again, about a foot. Mine was the only room this ever happened in. If we left the door open, nothing would happen. It was just left open then."

Other things puzzled the whole family. "We would see to it that the kitchen was cleaned up and the table cleared before we went to bed. In the night, some of us would hear the kitchen table being set. Sure enough, when we got up in the morning and went down to the kitchen, we'd find the table set for the whole family, just as it would be if one of us had set it, everything in its right place. Someone thought maybe Mother couldn't sleep and just got up to set the table for something to do to take up her time, but she said she never did."

"One night," Jack went on, "we were all sitting in the kitchen except Dad, who wasn't home that evening. Mother, Uncle Sy, my sister, and I were sitting around reading or studying our Sunday School lessons or whatever.

"Someone - I forget who it was - looked out the window toward the barn and saw what looked like someone carrying a kerosene lantern, from the barn to the house. We thought it was Dad coming home, that he had stopped in at the barn first.

"Sy and I went from the kitchen through a door into a side porch and then to the outside door. When we opened it, we heard the crunch of footsteps in the snow.

"Uncle Sy called out, 'Pete, is that you?' Everything disappeared - the lights and the sounds.

"There was a lantern in the porch. Uncle Sy lit it and went out in the yard to check if someone was out there.

When he got to the place, he could see footprints that came halfway from the barn to the house, and then just stopped. Not like most folks would stop, pulling one foot up even with the other while they stood still, but each footprint single and forward from the other. Then that was all. They weren't backtracked in, either. That was the only time that happened."

The other unexplainable happening also took place at night. Always at night. Other folks witnessed it, or at least tried to.

Many times,people heard violins playing in the grove near the house, and saw lights in the grove as though someone was carrying lanterns around out there. "This happened in winter, too," Jack explained, "so they weren't lightning bugs flying among the trees and grasses, or swamp gas lighting up as it met the heavy night air.

"It got so that people would come out from town and park in the road to listen. They'd turn their car lights off to watch for the mysterious, moving lights.

"We didn't have air conditioning then, and on some of those beastly hot nights some of us would take blankets out and lie there in the back yard until the house cooled off. Some of those nights, we would hear the music. It was as if the violins played the same song over and over and over, and then suddenly the music would end.

"The effect of those incidents stayed with me a long time. Later, our family moved to a big house in town. Whenever I went up to bed, I'd always stomp on the steps to scare the ghosts away.

"I don't have proof, but we were told that the Jesse James gang once stayed near our farm. Could their spirits have been haunting the grove from time to time, swinging their lanterns there in the night?"

My Father Cared

Dan Bartel told me about something that happened to him when he lived in a two-story house in LeRoy in Mower County, very close to the Iowa border.

His father died when Dan was sixteen, and he lived with his mother and sister. "When I was seventeen," he said, "I liked to play record albums and lie in bed listening to them. After the turntable automatically shut off, I would usually fall asleep.

"One warm Saturday night in May of 1972, I chose a favorite album and put it in place on the turntable. That night, the hall light was on because my sister had a girl friend spending the night. They were off downstairs somewhere when I went to bed.

"I apparently fell asleep while the album was still playing. My stereo was an older model and when it shut off the turntable made a loud click that woke me.

"When I opened my eyes, and then blinked and squinted a couple times, I saw two female figures staring down at me, both wearing something long and white. In the light from the hall, I could see their white hair, long and straight. When I sat up for a closer look, I could see that their hands and faces were also very pale.

"At first, I thought it must be my sister and her friend playing a joke on me. I thought they had powdered their own long, straight hair and maybe coated their faces and hands with some kind of stage makeup. Some joke!

"I didn't appreciate having my sleep disturbed that way. More angry than scared, I yelled, 'Get out of here!'

"They both backed slowly toward my bedroom doorway.

One moved out of my view into the hall. While the other passed through the doorway, I had a better look. With the hall light behind her that way, I could see she had no shoes or, for that matter, no feet either! The figure seemed to sort of float away and vanish.

"That was when I jumped out of bed and ran out into the hall, thinking if it was the girls, they had run down the hall to go downstairs. But no one was in the hall and no one was in my sister's room across the hall when I went by it.

"As I started for the stairs, I noticed Mother was still asleep in her room. So it had to be the girls. But if it was, how could they run down the hall and go downstairs without me hearing the steps squeak like they always did?

"It was starting to get to me. I didn't like what I was thinking - or rather couldn't think it through to a reasonable explanation. And no feet...how could a girl float like that?

"When I got downstairs, I searched the whole main floor. There wasn't anyone down there. This was getting a little scary.

"When I looked outside, the yard light was on, but my sister's car that should have been out there was nowhere in sight. My sister and her friend must have gone to town. So who was up in my room?

"I couldn't cope with this alone. I went up to Mother's room and woke her. When I told her what had happened, she kept calm but she acted like she knew more than she wanted to say. What she did say was, 'Dan, I don't know how to explain it so that you will understand. But it might help if you stay a few minutes after mass tomorrow to talk with our priest.'

"When I asked, 'What for, Mother? What does he have to do with this?' she said, 'Nothing, directly. But just tell him what happened and see what he thinks.'

"The next day, I did as Mother suggested. I felt awkward and a little foolish, but I stayed and visited with the priest. He seemed to know I was there for more than a casual visit. On his gentle prompting, I finally told him just what had happened. He said, 'Dan, the figures you saw were probably angels of God sent down by your father to check on you. He cared enough about his son to do that.'

"So that was it! Somehow, after that day, I felt closer to my father than I had while he was living. I knew for sure that he cared about me, even if he wasn't there to work with me or play catch with me. I knew my father cared, and everything would be all right from then on."

Flying Tumblers

The children had all grown up and left the nest. Sure, one or the other - and sometimes all eight at once - came home to Worthington now and then, and they called sometimes, but their mother still missed them. Especially when she was home alone. Or thought she was.

One day while Bob was at the VA Hospital, Lucille was enjoying the bright, sunny weather. Usually she didn't relish solitude, but this day was different. There was absolutely nothing gray or gloomy about it, so how could she feel anything but cheerful? Standing at the kitchen sink doing dishes again was routine. But this day she enjoyed routine more than usual.

Lucille lifted another glass from the sudsy water, gave it a good rinse, and set it on the towel to the right of the sink. That was where she always put the dishes until she put them back in the cabinet. While Lucille reached for a plate, the glass she had just set down on the towel suddenly flew up across the big kitchen, over the top of the round oak table in the center of the room and landed on the floor on the other side of the table. It didn't break.

"That really shook me up," she told Bob later.

When Lucille turned to look, she saw nothing that could have caused the glass to fly across the room. It wasn't even the kind of gray, spooky day that might make you think about scary things happening when you're in the house alone. But it made her remember another time, when Bob was at home. That time it was in the quiet, early evening. Lucille relaxed in the recliner in a corner of the living room. Bob lay on the sofa, turned so that he happened to be looking away from the action. He completely missed what happened.

Lucille had set a glass of water on the top of the step table next to the recliner when she sat down there. A few minutes later the glass flew up into the air and landed intact on the carpeted floor, the water still in it.

Lucille was startled. She asked, "Bob, did you see that?"

"Huh...what?...Oh, I dozed off. What are you talking about?"

"That glass, sitting there on the floor. I had it here on top of the table, and all of a sudden it just..." but Lucille gave up. Bob was snoring. Since he hadn't seen the glass airborne, being turned the other way, he didn't pay the least attention to what his wife was saying.

Lucille gingerly touched the glass. As she picked it up, she was thinking about a lot of possibilities. Did the spirit that lived with them on Nobles Street feel a bit lonesome now and then? Did it want a bit of attention in the quiet times? Did it miss the children who had talked and laughed and played and kept it company all those years, when they were still at home?

Grandpa's Hand

Diana Anderson of Windom shared something quite unusual that happened to her grandfather Doeden. She told me, "George Herman Doeden was my grandfather. I never knew him when he had both hands, but he was always very special to me and I loved him dearly.

"When I was a small girl, I was told that Grandpa had lost his hand in a threshing accident. I couldn't see that he even missed it, though. He always got along just fine and seemed to be able to do everything anyone else did. He had a hook he could use when he needed it, but I hardly ever saw him wear it.

"Grandpa would let me sit on his lap and touch the stump of his arm. I never thought of it as something to be scared of. It was so soft and I thought, 'How smooth!' But I also thought how it must have hurt him when he lost his hand. He must have been in his early twenties when it happened. After they got his hand out of the machine, they buried it in the cemetery at Worthington. I suppose it was his parents who buried it. And I used to think about that.

"I knew that when people died, they were buried in a cemetery. I decided that the cemetery was also a logical place to bury a dead, useless part of a living person, like Grandpa's hand. And it seemed a more proper way of taking care of it than just discarding it.

"Only thing was, when they buried Grandpa's hand, they didn't know it would make a difference how they placed it in the ground.

"As the weeks went by and the stump healed, Grandpa kept feeling his hand as if it was still there. They say that's not unusual. It has something to do with the nerves. But there was more to it than *that* with Grandpa. He said it was more like his hand was there and was uncomfortable, but he couldn't move it or make it more comfortable, because it wasn't really there. That caused him a lot of distress.

"Someone who heard about his trouble told him, 'You must dig up the hand and lay it at rest with the palm down. Then it will rest easy.'

"So they dug up the hand and turned it over and buried it again, palm down. After that, Grandpa was greatly relieved because the sensation of his hand always being there but not being comfortable, was gone. His hand could rest easier, and so could he.

"Grandpa just went right on doing about everything anyone else could do. The only thing that was different was that I thought about what had happened. I thought about it a whole lot. Now and then, I even visited that special place in the cemetery. Though my imagination might have conjured up horror scenes of a hand reaching up from a grave, I left that for the movies. As I said, his hand was resting easy now, and he wasn't troubled by it anymore. I accepted that, and nothing about it ever haunted either of us later."

Serenity Disrupted

Diana Anderson of Windom tells another tale.

It was one of those golden days in southwest Minnesota during bow season, a day to enjoy the serenity of the woods. Stealthy moves were the order of the day if you hoped to sneak up on a deer.

Fourteen-year-old Dwayne started the early morning with alertness and enthusiasm. By the time he left the old van, though, he had calmed himself as he knew the importance of keeping quiet.

Diana, Dwayne's mother, looked forward to the annual event when she and her parents and her son went hunting together. She hoped her son, like her, would know what to do if he was lucky enough to walk up on a deer.

This time Diana's mother, Frieda, couldn't join the party. She had to help serve a luncheon at the church, and she couldn't be sure she would get there in time if she went to the woods first. Diana's father, Roy Doeden, was getting along in years. He was content to stay at his stand while the other two took turns walking the hills to drive the deer toward him.

As he leaned against a sturdy cottonwood tree, Roy thought of other years when *he* was the young fellow that went on ahead and scared up the deer. He recalled the time he couldn't bring himself to watch while the men dressed one out. To him, the deer were beautiful creatures that belonged in the plains and woodlands on his father's farm. He thought of their rich, warm-toned coats and the startled look in the eyes of a yearling he had once faced.

Lost in his thoughts, Roy realized it had been almost two hours now since Dwayne had gone off on his own. Had he gotten sidetracked imagining what life was like for the settlers along the Des Moines River when the Indians hunted and lived here? He'll be back soon enough, Roy thought, and he'll be wanting one of these big pecan rolls.

Turning his back against the sun filtering through the treetops, Roy heard movement nearby. He raised his bow and waited, but it was Dwayne and Diana coming in for lunch.

"I didn't see a thing, Dad," Diana said, "except a squirrel scurrying around in the leaves and a mink snooping around an old log. How are *you* doing?"

"Me? I'm all right. Nothing moving in the woods today," Roy said as he poured some steaming coffee into the thermos top and set it down to cool.

"I wouldn't say that, Gramps," Dwayne said. "I walked to the high lines...and then I turned back and walked as far as that clearing at Comstock's, across from where Fort Belmont used to be. I saw something and it wasn't a deer. I'm not sure what it was I did see."

Diana asked, "What happened?"

"I wish I knew." Dwayne struggled to calm himself. He sat down and reached for a roll, but then put it back in the bag.

"What's the matter?" Diana said. "What happened? Was there someone down by the river? Is there something Dad and I ought to know?"

Finally Dwayne told his story. "I was walking carefully, so's not to rustle the leaves or break a twig. And I didn't hear any other sounds around me, either. I sneaked up and down a couple of the knolls. Then I went up that steepest rise and started down the other slope toward the river. All the while I looked around me and through the brush ahead, watching for a deer. Every now and then, I stood still so I could catch any sound in the woods, watching for either a pair of ears or a white tail showing above the undergrowth.

"When I got to the river bank, I turned and looked up the path I'd just come down and..."

"What?" asked his mother.

"You probably won't believe this, but about 40 feet away, on the path I had just come down, was an old lady."

"A lady? All by herself? What would an old woman be doing in these hills, alone?"

"You tell me. I have no idea."

"What did you do?"

"It sounds crazy now, but I said, 'Good morning.'"

"And? What did she say?"

"Nothing. She turned her body toward me, and that was when I could see she didn't have a face! It was weird! She was kind of short, and she was wearing a long, draggy dark dress. And she had on a black bonnet. Where her face should have been, there was...nothing! No mask, no bones, no cavities like in a skull...just sort of a blank. I can't even describe it. She carried a basket on her arm. Her dress was so old fashioned...like a pioneer woman might have worn."

Diana said, "What did you do?"

"I stood there like a dummy while she walked away. No...not walked. She didn't really walk. She sort of drifted or glided, you could say - and just a little above the ground, too. I didn't hear a sound when she went by me.

And that was when I ran back here as fast as I could, and I didn't even look back down to see where she went, or if I could still see her. I must have lost at least three arrows while I was running."

Roy had been taking it all in without speaking. Finally he said, "Well, what you saw is not impossible, when you think about it. Right down there near the river bank there used to be an old Indian burial mound, so Indians camped near here or passed through here, or roamed these woods looking for food. The women would have gone out to gather berries. As a matter of fact, so would the early settlers. Your description fits a pioneer woman best."

"But, Grampa, that was so long ago. What are you telling me?"

"It might have been a pioneer woman, long laid to rest, who for some reason unknown to us is *not* at rest. Her spirit could wander here for almost any reason. My guess is that she's looking for a loved one who died here somewhere, long ago."

"Let's find a different place to hunt after we eat, okay?"

Some Kind of Spirit

After Aunt Susan departed this life, she stayed close to her niece, Beth, who felt that her aunt's spirit was near and was aware of Beth's needs. Beth felt comfortable with it and shared her experiences with her brother.

One fall when school was about to start again, Beth naturally wondered how that first day would go. How many kids would be there? How many of them would be bullies? Would she know anyone? Could she sit by her brother? What would the new teacher be like?

While Beth was walking near the school, some time before opening day, someone who looked like Aunt Susan came to Beth and said, "Come. I'll show you the new teacher." Aunt Susan had just sort of appeared. The door never opened, but there was Aunt Sue as if she had come through the wall. Beth remembers looking at the wall of the school then, and looking back at their house and thinking: I'm not dreaming then. These are real things. But it's hard to figure out where I am and how that happened. I'm sort of seeing it all from up above it.

The teacher had on a green dress with big, brown leaves in the print. Beth noticed her hair, too, because she had a bushy perm. She called Beth 'Jeanette.' Beth thought she must remind the teacher of a former student.

The next morning as they walked to school, Beth and her brother were talking about the new teacher. Beth said, "She'll be wearing a green dress with big, brown leaves."

Her brother asked, "How do you know what she's wearing?"

"Aunt Susan told me that, and she showed me the new

teacher, too. And that's what she had on."

Beth started thinking back to when she was younger. She recalled that Aunt Susan had come to her in her bedroom at home a few times, but she wasn't visiting in their house at the time. Then Beth thought of the time Aunt Sue had on a new coat, and she took it off and covered Beth with it. The next morning, when Beth went out to the kitchen for breakfast, she asked, "Is Aunt Susan up yet?"

As Mother buttered the toast, she answered, "I couldn't possibly know that. Why are you asking?"

"I want to thank her for covering me with her new coat last night."

Mother looked Beth in the eye and seemed to be thinking about what to say. What she did say was, "You were dreaming."

Later Beth and her brother always thought of Aunt Susan as a fairy godmother or a guardian angel. She had to be. What else? They had been at her funeral and had watched while her casket was lowered into the gaping rectangle. She had to be *some kind of spirit*, to come back like that.

A Hanging Phone

Matt started his story this way: "Michael was my dad. When he was seventeen, he was doing field work. One day in early August, he was out cultivating a cornfield for the last time that season. About 8:30 p.m., he stopped for the day. He turned off the tractor and left it and the cultivator in the middle of the field, where the next day's work would start. Then he began to walk home, about two miles across the fields.

"Between the field and the farmyard, there was Vang Lutheran Church. It was one of those old rural churches about 125 years old. It was between Northfield and Dennison, a town of fewer than 200 inhabitants. In those days, according to Dad, church doors were usually left unlocked. Folks who needed to go in to pray or to seek help could do so, he told me.

"So as Dad walked past the church, he decided to go into the church to call his girl friend, Debra. She was home, and they talked for a long time. At about 9:15 and nearly pitch dark, while he was still in the church basement talking on the phone, he heard someone talking upstairs. He listened, and he heard other voices. He could see there were no lights on up there, so he figured there wasn't any meeting or anything.

"He asked Debra to hold on while he checked out the voices. He went up the steps about halfway so he could listen at the chapel doors and pushed one door open just enough to make a little crack. It was dark in there. He couldn't see anyone, but he heard sort of a voice. He couldn't identify it or understand the words. He waited, but saw no sign of anyone in the chapel.

"He let the door close. Then he went back down to the phone to talk to Deb some more. As soon as he did, he heard the strange voice again. He kept talking to Debra and told her about it again. Then he heard the voice come down the steps toward the basement area. He saw a faded blur, not like someone walking, but more like sliding or floating. He told Debra he would run home and she should call his house in exactly five minutes. If he wasn't home by then, she was to call his parents and tell them where he called from. All this while, he was still hearing the voice. He hung up the phone as he bounded up the stairs and out the door.

"Choosing the shortest way, Dad ran frantically, through trees and brush, getting scratched by branches and tripped by roots. When he reached his house, the phone was ringing. There was no one home to answer it. He stumbled up the porch steps and in to the phone. His father was calling to ask him if he had finished cultivating that field. When he heard how out of breath his son was, he asked if he was okay.

"Michael, my dad, told his father what had happened. They picked Debra up and they all went to the church. They found nothing out of place or missing, except that the phone was hanging off the hook. And the chapel doors, usually closed, stood wide open."

A Warm Spot

When people are telling about their ghosts, they sometimes say, "We have a cold spot in our house." That's no surprise to those who have read books about ghosts; the cold spot is believed to be the spot where the spirit enters or leaves.

Holly and her husband believe they had a ghost. Neither of them ever saw it, but they felt that where it had stood, unlike others, it left a *warm* place. As Holly tells it, "We never saw our ghost, but we felt where it had stood. This happened at least six times."

She described their home as an old two-story house south of Atwater. Their upstairs bedroom had linoleum on the floor. "That was probably why we could feel the difference in temperature so well. That room had only a small wall heater, so the linoleum floor was always cold," she said.

"One night," Holly continued, "as I got ready for bed, I felt a warm place beneath my bare feet. I moved around on it to check it out. It was round, about like a large dinner plate. At first I thought our small house dog had been lying there, but then I realized he would never lie on that cold linoleum, even if he was upstairs. He'd either be on our bed, on the girls' bed, or in his room, which was a closet.

"Quite a while later, the warm spot appeared again. From the locations of the spots, it seemed that our ghost preferred our bedroom and it hovered around either by the side or the foot of our bed, except once when the door stood open. Then it was behind the door.

"I thought I'd check it out. I crouched down and tried

to feel the spot with my hands. That didn't work. But with my bare feet, it did. It was always a very definite warm, round area, always the same size. I asked Lee if he had just been standing there, but I knew that was a foolish question. It wasn't that simple.

"The second time we felt it, we worried about a fire. But there apparently was no short in the wiring below the floor. We wondered if there was an animal's nest between the floor and ceiling, and we were feeling their body heat. But we never heard anything. Later, we tore the old house down. The wiring was just fine. And there was no sign of a nest."

When they reflected on it, both Holly and Lee realized they had felt the warm spots only in the evenings. Now they live in a new home with carpeted floors and ceiling heat. But they haven't felt any warm spots as in the other house. One unexplainable thing does happen in the new house, though. They'll be sitting in the dining room when all of a sudden Lee's guitar will twang in the living room. In the evenings.

The couple are wondering if the ghost has changed its tactics to make its presence known in the new environment, perhaps because now that the floors are carpeted, it can't shed warmth on one spot as easily as it could on that cold linoleum floor. Or does the carpeting just make it harder for Holly and Lee to feel the warm spots?

A Host of... Ghosts?

It was late Saturday afternoon when a stranger found the graveyard on the edge of a small town in southwestern Minnesota. He parked his S-10 at the end of the long gravel lane. He noticed that the cemetery was in the middle of a cornfield. "Good! I'll be alone," he thought. Alone to explore the cemetery. He had his own reasons to do that.

He noticed a sign pointing toward the river. "Historical Marker," it said. "Must be a pioneer cabin site down there on the bank of the Des Moines," he thought.

He climbed the fence at the far corner of the burial ground and found the path down through the woods. There he found a grassy depression marked as the cabin site. All that was left now was the low spot and a few big rocks that could have been the cabin's foundation corners. And small trees were beginning to crowd in on the site.

It was quiet down there, except for the squirrels scurrying through the old layers of leaves underfoot and from one tree to another. He watched the river as it flowed on down toward where it widened and tumbled over a rocky bed.

He sat on one of the smooth rocks and tried to feel what it would have been like, there along the river in pioneer times...arriving...choosing a site...maybe living in the wagon or under the propped wagon cover until a sod shanty or a cabin could be built...clearing the timber to use for firewood and to make room for a garden...breaking the sod beyond the woods to prepare the ground for planting crops in the spring...

A sound interrupted his thoughts. A car door slamming?

"Oh-oh...I sat here and forgot all about my pickup and the back's not locked. I sure don't want anyone snooping around in it."

In less than a minute, he reached the fence and saw that a group of teenagers and a woman, maybe their teacher or supervisor, had come. As he climbed back over the fence, he saw that some of them entered the cemetery by the steps, up and down again, while others opened the gate to walk in. He heard them laughing at each other. The stranger thought, "Sounds like they believe the old story, that one who died a natural death was worthy and could be carried in through the gateway. One who took his own life was carried up over the steps and down."

His response to their cheerful greeting was curt. He pretended to be scrutinizing the few tombstones that were still there, while the kids picked up the debris left by the wind or by careless visitors. Candy bar wrappers, greasy waxed bags, styrofoam cups, sandwich and pizza boxes, plastic forks, leaves, pop and beer cans. The cans went into a "We Recycle" container, the leaves into another, and all the rest into a trash bag.

"These are good kids," he realized. "They're into recycling and they're volunteering their time for cleanup."

As he turned to another marker, the woman asked, "Can we help you? These 4-H-ers have been here a lot and they know as much about who's buried here - even in the graves missing markers - as anyone does."

He had to be civil and say something, but he hesitated. "Uh...no, I think I've found what I was looking for. This monument is of special interest to me." He continued to run his fingertips along the worn lines of the inscription.

He pretended to be writing something on a card and showed no interest in further conversation.

The 4-H club leader went back to her crew. They finished the clean-up back in the fence corners. Commenting on the missing tombstones, they picked up their containers and tossed them into the pickup box before they jumped in. They started back to town, leaving the man there alone.

But their drivers' thoughts were confused. As she drove, LuAnn Surecross wondered what the man's connection to that one stone was. All he said was that it was "of special interest" to him. She wished he had said more. Maybe there was some history of the area connected to him or that marker.

The next day's *Argus Leader* carried a feature about unique hobbies. One caught her attention. "Some collectors," the article said, "have even gone so far as to collect gravestones to make their patio floors." No names were given, no addresses.

What a weird hobby, LuAnn thought. I hope those patios are a long ways from here. Who would want to walk on tombstones, or sit in a patio chair and sip lemonade while reading those names and dates, reminders of people long gone? After all, they were someone's family! It would be morbid. Those collectors must be sick.

It nagged at her that the stranger in the cemetery had acted as he did, volunteering no name or connection to the area. She got into the pickup and drove out to the cemetery. She opened the gate and found the far row of markers. The "interesting" tombstone was gone.

So that's what he was up to! I'll bet he waited around

until we left, and then took that stone - he probably had a crowbar or something in that pile of stuff in his truck - and hauled it away. Sure, he did. Here's where he dragged it through the gate to where his truck was parked. Now I wish I'd taken his license number. But I had no idea... There are few enough of the original markers left as it is, below these white wooden crosses.

And that's not the whole story. LuAnn may never know who the man was or where his patio proclaims the birth and death dates of Murray County pioneers, entirely out of their home area and final resting place. But the stranger will know. And he will be troubled forever. Not by his conscience. Apparently he has none. But The Legend will follow him. The Legend the kids all know and believe - that a host of heavenly spirits will hover protectively over the final resting places of the dead, and if a tombstone is disturbed, *A Host of Ghosts* will follow the stone and forever appear over it in its new resting place. It will prevent any peaceful rest for the one who removed it.

What a surprise he's in for, LuAnn thought. His patio with its unique floor will allow him no relaxation. I didn't get his license number, but I'll let *The Host of Ghosts* see to him and give him his reward!

Fertile Soil for Ghost Stories

A young woman working at KWOA Radio Station west of Worthington around Halloween had heard of a ghost in the Lamberton area. That led to a ghost-story hunt. Lamberton wasn't hard to find. It's between Walnut Grove and New Ulm on Highway 14 going east and west, just a few miles west of Highway 71 going north and south between Jeffers and Redwood Falls.

Lamberton is in a very historical area. One can visit the place where Laura Ingalls Wilder once lived and played at Walnut Grove. There is also the McCone sod house, a reconstructed pioneer home of the 1880's, near Sanborn. The Harkin Store and the monument to the massacred settlers at New Ulm are not far away. There's also the Lower Sioux Indian Reservation and related sites near Redwood Falls and Morton. South of Sanborn are the Jeffers Petroglyphs.

The story told around Lamberton has to do with a grave on top of a hill just outside the town, not far from the four-way stop called Sanborn Corners, where 14 and 71 intersect. It is said that a young girl of about twelve years of age was buried alive in that grave on the hill, and that her ghost has been seen in the area. If she was buried alive, one can conclude that her spirit is not at peace. Some folks claim to have seen her wandering alone on the hill at night. Others say they have heard her moan and whimper as she hovers around that four-way stop. There seems to be some agreement as to the spirit being that of a young girl, though some say she hovers and others say she can only be heard, never seen.

Another Lamberton area story revolves around three Indian women who were buried on a hill on land that has been farmed over for years. Those who pass over the spot as they work the soil think about the three women and wonder if their spirits roam there. "The Three Maidens" is a familiar symbol and site in the Native American culture, especially in legends of nearby Pipestone, so it's natural food for thought.

There was once a City of Sanborn Cemetery, so it is no surprise that the tales abound. There was a time when all the graves were moved to the new Sanborn City Cemetery, but for some reason one marker was left behind. That marker, roughly three feet high and two feet wide and made of iron, was close to the line that separated two farms. After being shifted from one side of the fence to the other in the regular routine of farming near it, it was finally placed on the exact fenceline.

When Sanborn celebrated its Centennial, the facts about the old and new cemeteries were published. The articles told that one remaining marker had not been moved with the others. Perhaps that would have been better left unsaid, for it drew attention to the site of the old cemetery and the one remaining marker, which was promptly stolen from its place and was never returned.

One person commented that the old cemetery land would never be farmed because the area is rocky and full of holes where the old graves were, and the holes are grown full of weeds. Nor would it be good for exploring, because one could fall into an empty grave. But it sounds like a good place for ghosts to haunt - ghosts of young girls, Indian women, or whomever. And it is fertile ground for ghosts and ghost stories, if you can unearth them.

Farewell from the Fog

Larry Rogers' maternal grandfather, John Telford, ran an oil distributorship. He lived in Pipestone most of his life, in a big, two-story house at the end of an alley until his death in 1957. Larry's mother and several of her siblings grew up in that house and, Larry said, "Grandpa John Telford retired there."

He added, "Grandpa couldn't walk real well anymore, the last years of his life. He was seen walking down that alley many times, but always very slowly."

Several nights after John's death, his widow was having trouble sleeping. No matter how tired she was, she'd be up prowling around in the house. She would call her daughter at any hour of the night to talk with her when sleep wouldn't come. Larry said, "Grandma's house and my mother's were only a block apart, but for some reason Mother hesitated to walk that alley at night. She preferred to talk with Grandma over the phone, to try to calm her down. So even when Grandma called and asked her to come over, Mother usually stayed where she was.

"This went on for two or three weeks after Grandpa's death. One night, Mother gave in and went over to Grandma's. When she had walked down the alley about three-fourths of the way, she experienced a sudden haze or fog. She didn't think much about it, just noticed it.

"There were a few other nights after that when she pleased Grandma by walking over to talk. On a couple of those nights, a fog appeared, but while it seemed to be a few feet thick at first, it seemed to diminish each night.

"The last night Mother walked down there to try to calm

Grandma down so they could both get to sleep again, she found the fog was there again. It didn't prevent her from walking on, but this time it surprised her. She saw Grandpa standing in it and waving to her.

"Mother walked the rest of the way to Grandma's house, all the while turning around and trying to decide what she really saw. When she got to Grandma's, she walked into the kitchen. There she found Grandma sound asleep at the table, with her feet up on a chair, perfectly relaxed.

"That night marked the end to the nightly phone calls, the end to Mother's hesitant walks down the alley, and the end to Grandma's restlessness. From then on, she could sleep peacefully. It was as though John Telford said his last goodbye that night. No one, including Mother, ever experienced the fog in the alley afterward.

"Mother told me the story when I was in my early teens, and I accepted it. Mother was always frail physically, but she was mentally astute. I think she always believed she saw Grandpa's ghost in that fog."

Meet Molly

Mabel said things started happening shortly after her family moved into the house. Things they weren't expecting, such as window sashes going up and down when no one was opening or closing them. Or pull-down ceiling fixtures coming down from the ceiling and sometimes going up again.

At first, the family thought it was because their three-story home was one of the older houses in their town in Nobles County. The windows and fixtures might certainly have been old, because the house was over a hundred years old, but when the family tried to open those same windows purposely, they were very hard to push up.

One night when a couple of the girls were in their second-floor bedroom, "I told them to turn their light off and go to bed," Mabel said. "A little while later, I noticed their light was still on, so I told them again to turn it off. When one of the girls called out, 'Mother, *we* didn't turn it on,' I wondered who was responsible.

"After the incidents with the music boxes, we began to speak freely of our ghost. What happened with the music boxes was that I woke up about three a.m. to hear the music box on the baby's crib playing. It just kept playing, over and over, with no one there rewinding it. When I checked, the baby was sound asleep at the other end of the crib. Sometimes other music boxes on the girls' dressers played, too.

"After that, different members of the family said they often felt like someone else was around, but they never felt afraid of the presence. We just accepted it. From then on, when something unexplainable happened, the person it happened to would usually just go back to sleep. No big deal.

"Some of us heard footsteps, usually at night. One night, my two oldest sons came home. From the TV room on the first floor, they heard footsteps on second floor. When they went upstairs to check on who was there, they heard the footsteps again - but now they were on the third floor. They went up there, but didn't find anyone. When they went back down to first floor, the footsteps started again on the floor above them. Everyone else in the house was sound asleep. The ones sleeping in the two third-floor bedrooms slept through it all.

"Once when three of the children were on second floor, they came running down to tell me, 'There's a lady's face on the wall in the hallway. She looks old. She has a wrinkled face and white hair. All we can see is her face.' I went up to look, but didn't see anything like that. I guess that face they saw confirmed our belief that our ghost was a 'she.' From then on, we all called her Molly.

"Several years later, one of the girls sleeping on third floor woke up one night and saw a face on the ceiling. She woke her sister, who looked at the face and said, 'That's the same face we saw downstairs on the hall wall' and then she pulled the covers up over her head in fright. She said later that she peeked out every now and then until the face was gone, whereas her sister, who woke up first, had already turned over and gone back to sleep.

"Another night, when those two older boys and a friend were watching a late movie on TV, they heard footsteps coming down the open stairway in the hall. At the bottom step, the footsteps turned to the front door. The boys couldn't see anyone there, but from the TV room they saw the front door open and close. That door had never closed easily, but it was closed when they checked it.

"Their friend was so scared he wouldn't go out that door to go home, so he stayed all night.

"One other night, I didn't know what woke me. I thought it was the cat. Our cat wouldn't use a litter box, but she would wake someone to let her out. Usually I left the bedroom door wide open so I could hear the kids, and I left a night light on in the bathroom. Like I said, I thought it was the cat that woke me. I called her name, but she didn't jump up on the bed. I put my hand down beside the bed to see if she was there. What I felt was definitely not the cat. I felt coldness radiating toward my hand, just as if someone had just come in from out in the cold. I said, 'Who's there?' and then I heard footsteps from the other side of the bed go around to the side where the door was. The door opened, but there wasn't enough light to see anyone go out of the room. Then I realized that, although I had left the door open as usual, it had somehow been closed again that night, until that moment.

"I got up to check on who could have been up. Everyone was asleep. The outside doors were all locked. I decided it was Molly, and I went back to sleep.

"On third floor, there's a door into a storage space under the eaves. In the mornings, the kids would find that door open. They started to set a chair against it when they went to bed, but in the mornings the chair would be moved to one side and the door would be open. It was almost as if some unknown guest frequented that storage space, but we couldn't see any evidence. We just credited Molly with all the strange happenings.

"One night the girls whose rooms were at the southeast side of the house heard sounds of a party out in the back yard. They woke me, but no one was out there.

"Gradually, our ghost left us. At least, we heard no footsteps or music that we couldn't account for. No doors opened or closed mysteriously. The children saw no more faces on the wall or ceiling. But when Molly was gone, we all felt her absence. Something was missing.

"Later on, one of the girls came up with a theory as to what ended it. She said, 'Mom, do you remember when Dad filled the old caved-in cistern and well and cemented over them? I'll bet that locked the ghost in there. Those must have been her old daytime haunts, and now she can't get out at night and haunt us any more in the house.'"

But Mabel said that the daughter who came up with that theory wasn't so confident when Mabel reminded her, "But have you noticed? That cement's starting to crack."

Finding the Missing Paper

Manford Theel of Paynesville in Stearns County said that every word of his story is true. He told of the good life his grandfather on his mother's side had lived. William Arndt had been a Sunday school superintendent, had led prayer meetings, and had even preached if the minister was away. Arndt was also a bank director, insurance agent, and assessor. Because folks knew he was an upright citizen and could be trusted, many people asked him for help with minor legal problems. He was often named as executor of estates.

That's how he happened to be involved with the Giesel family. They were neighbors of his, and when Mr. Giesel died in about 1939, Arndt was executor of the estate. Two years later, in 1941, Arndt also died.

Manford Theel said that when he and Arlene married in 1944, his folks moved to town and he and Arlene lived on the farm. Along toward fall that year, a letter came from an heir of the Giesel estate. The letter explained that they had never received the last paper, the discharge of personal representative or executor form, that signed Arndt off as executor of the estate. Manford said that his mother, Sadie, wrote to the people, telling them that Grandpa Arndt had died and that his family didn't know anything about the estate settlement.

They wrote back, saying that they had discovered oil on some property in Canada and they had to have this final paper to give them clear title in the oil rights. They said the paper had to be among Arndt's things.

Manford, Arlene, and Manford's folks all looked

through Grandpa Arndt's brief case with its many leather compartments. They could find nothing relating to the Giesel estate. Manford had Arndt's roll-top writing desk out on the farm. He and Arlene even took the top off, thinking the paper could have fallen behind or in it somewhere. It wasn't there.

By this time, Sadie had received another letter stating that the missing paper had been mailed from the Stearns County Court House in St. Cloud and that it must be there somewhere. "My mother was a very kind-hearted person," Manford Theel said. "She would help rather than hurt anyone. She searched again. She got so she even walked the floor thinking about it, so one day we all started looking for it all over again. We didn't find it.

"The next morning," he said, "my father came out to help with the chores and the milking. He startled me with his news. He said, 'We found the paper.'

"I asked him where in the world it had been. He said that about two o'clock in the night, Mother started talking in her sleep. At least, that's what he thought she was doing. She said, 'What do you want?' and she sat up on the side of the bed in a cold sweat. Ruben asked her what was the matter. She said, 'My dad was here.'

"Ruben asked her jokingly, still thinking she was talking in her sleep, 'What did he want?'

"Mother answered, very much awake, 'He came right through the wall. First he spoke my name in a low tone. Then he called it out more loudly. The third time, he spoke sharply, calling out my name. Then when he knew he had my attention, he told me the papers we were still looking for were way back in his folder brief case, as he had always called it. Then he was gone.'

"Mother got out of bed. She walked to the closet and got out the folder. She gave a little tug, and the last compartment, way in the back of it, opened. And there was the paper!"

Manford Theel believes the spirits of the dead can see what we are doing here on earth. The experience with the search for the missing paper, with the help of William Arndt, deceased, made Manford a believer. "I want to be with the good spirits, if any," he concluded.

Academic Ghosts

Several institutions of higher learning in central and west central Minnesota have their ghosts.

Some, like those at Concordia Moorhead, are so young that they are not yet considered legendary, but Stearns County colleges have legendary ghosts. Kevin Britz wrote their stories for the October 1989 and 1990 issues of the Stearns County Historical Society's publication, *Crossings*.

Britz says there are variations of the familiar stories; the best one started during the building of the Abbey Church of St. John's in the 1880s.

St. John's was fairly young, established as a school for men in St. Cloud in 1857 and moved to Collegeville in 1867.

The story goes that the mother of a young monk who died of a fall from a scaffold, vowed to return, when the Abbot wouldn't listen to her demands for an explanation. When the building was finished, the mother again confronted the Abbot at the dedication, but he had her removed from the building. She left, promising to return, but on her way home she drowned when her buggy turned over, spilling her into one of the lakes near the campus.

Strange occurrences after that seem to be related. They included doors suddenly opening and wet footprints appearing in the center aisle of the church. Eventually, a new church was dedicated. Though neither the mother nor her ghost appeared bodily, a crack formed down the center aisle of the new church on the day of the dedication. Her son, the monk was born in 1849, so his mother would have been somewhere around 130 years old by that time, a goodly age to have become a spirit.

Another St. John's University ghost tale concerns a young monk whose boat overturned in 1890 in Sagatagon Lake when he was taking stone to the chapel for its construction. Britz says that Brother Anselm Bartolome and a student named Felix Nelles were hauling stone to the Stella Maris Chapel. When the boat overturned, Brother Anselm panicked. Nelles went under, but finally freed himself from Bartolome and made it to shore; Bartolome drowned. Perhaps it is his spirit folks hear splashing in the lake, or maybe it is his ghost who has been seen, robed in black, leaving wet footprints in the halls and cells.

Then there is the tale of the bear named Murro, once a pet at St. John's. Murro had the run of the campus for a while, but one day a student teased Murro, who chased him into Lake Sagatagon. Though the student climbed into a boat, grabbed an oar, and hit the bear with it, the bear reached the boat and maimed the student. As a result, Murro was killed in order to end the danger of further attacks. Since then, students have reported that as they walked on the paths around the lake, they have seen a student with his face and neck bleeding, being chased toward the lake by a "spectral bear," as Britz tells it. But when they follow them to the lake, they find no bear, no bleeding student.

Stories told at Frank House, a dorm at St. John's University, are related to a student suicide long ago. The spirit of that student uses the same methods that are used in other dorms on other campuses: voices come from empty rooms; lights, radios and TVs are turned on or off; and doors are closed and faucets turned on at night when all students are asleep. But at Frank House, no one has seen a ghostly face or a floating, filmy substance or a hooded, cloaked figure.

The nearby College of St. Benedict, established for women in 1912 at St. Joseph, also has its ghosts. One is the ghost of a young nun who died and was buried in the convent cemetery. She appears from time to time so that she can comfort students passing the cemetery who might be discouraged enough to consider ending their own lives.

Another of St. Ben's stories has to do with a secret room that no one can locate. Britz says that in this story, a student who had been sick for a long time died in that room. Later, students occupying the room heard "sounds of moaning and screaming." Understandably, the room wasn't used for a number of years. Finally, a student tried living in it, but when the sounds were again heard, the building administrator had the room walled off. But now, no one can seem to locate it.

According to Britz, there is also haunting at nearby St. Cloud State University, started in 1866 as a coeducational teachers' college. A spectral woman in high heels walks down the corridors of Riverview, the second-oldest building on the campus. Footsteps have been heard at various times, years apart, by reputable professors and custodians. But no one has seen the ghostly figure responsible.

It is interesting that the ghost of Riverview at St. Cloud closely resembles the ghost of Larsen Hall at Luther College in Decorah, Iowa. There, in the section of the building used as the college health service, heels are heard clicking down the hall at night when all other offices are closed. A part of the third floor of Luther's Larsen Hall is frequented by "Gertrude," blamed for setting off the fire alarm at midnight, or leaving dresser and desk drawers open, where clothes are missing or replaced with her clothes of an earlier era.

Such is the stuff that academic ghosts are made of.

A Ghost in the Drain?

A college student doesn't need surprises. Well, pleasant ones might be welcome, but not unpleasant ones such as those reported at Hoyum, a girls' dorm at Concordia College in Moorhead.

Picture a freshman girl getting ready for a date. She looks in the mirror above the washbowls and sees a hooded and caped figure behind her, reflected in the mirror. Or she looks out from the shower to see the mysterious figure hovering just above the shower door. Definitely not a welcome surprise.

Or think of a student who has attended all her classes, endured a full hour of orchestra rehearsal, and then worked in the cafeteria line to earn her board. She's tired, but she has to study a good three and a half hours in a dorm full of girls before she can go to bed.

Then, more than ready for sleep, she climbs up to her loft and flops down. She reaches to pull up her blanket. There, at the foot of her bed, on the same ladder she just climbed up seconds ago, is the horrid figure. She is sure the door was locked when she returned to her room after supper. No one was there when she came back from the bathroom. Was there a ghost in the dorm? The girls concluded that there *was*. They have proof.

Sometimes students who are known for their neat rooms will find them all out of order, clothing and books and papers strewn all over the floor. Locked doors open slowly in the early evening hours. Or radios and TVs are blaring when their owners are sure they had turned them off when they left their rooms. Sometimes, even in midwinter when the heat is on in the rooms and halls, a cold draft or a cold spot will be felt, always in the same part of the same rooms. Some of the girls wake up to their names being called out, but there's no one around and the hall is perfectly quiet.

Probably the most alarming incident on Hoyum's fifth floor made the girls wonder if their ghost liked water, lots of it. Or maybe lived in the bathtub drain and sewer lines. A bathtub faucet flooded their bathroom with hot water. Not once, but three times in a month.

Two inches of water on a bathroom floor and gallons of it seeping out under the door and into the carpeted hall is not a trick students would play on each other, especially when on their return from mid-semester break they had to work those first two hours sopping up the water or pay someone to bring in a wet-dry vac to clean up the rest of the water. One would hardly think the students enjoyed the mopping and the expense enough to cause the flood the second and third times. It had to be a ghost!

The girls were convinced. They agreed to be on the alert for proof, so that others could also be made to believe that Concordia's Hoyum Hall also had a ghost, though it was not yet widely known.

Not Ready Yet

Rosie was used to having things her way while she lived in the pleasant, light green ranch house in a town in Lyon County. Although her husband had died many years earlier, she prided herself on still being able to take care of the property by herself. Neat and orderly. That was the way Rosie liked things. Neighbors said that while she lived there alone, she always had everything "just so" or, as some said, "in apple pie order." The woman wasn't really alone. She had many memories of the good years while her husband lived. And she had good neighbors.

Speaking of good neighbors, Rosie herself was one. She was much appreciated by Jon and Karen who lived just around the corner. They said that when they looked out their windows, they would see her pick up apples from under the tree in their yard. Then she would make them into apple pies, which she gave them. Jon said, "It was her gift of the pies that made us think of her as a good neighbor."

Eventually Rosie died in her house, in the bathroom, of an apparent heart attack. No more apple pies. After her death, the house was unoccupied for almost a year before a family bought it.

The new occupants had been settled in for only a short while when the gentleman came to Karen's door asking, "Do you know if there's a locksmith in town? We've tried everything, but we can't get the bathroom door open."

Karen said, "We could probably find one listed in the yellow pages, but let me come over first and see if I can help." When she went over, Karen could see that they had indeed tried everything to the point of marring the door and frame. She recognized the type of lock. It was one of those that can be locked from inside the bathroom by pushing in the little metal peg.

"But no one's in the bathroom," the new owner said. "How did the door get locked?"

Karen thought, "But you don't know the half of it," while she bent a wire coat hanger open until she had a straight end. She poked the wire into the hole until it hit the button and pushed it back to its unlocked position. The door opened without any further trouble. But what she said before she left did trouble the owner considerably. He couldn't figure out what she meant by saying, "Rosie probably wasn't ready to come out yet."

A Face from the Past

Nathan Swenson of New London lives in a house that had once been a two-story depot on the Burlington Northern. Before he lived there, numerous others had made their home in the converted depot. It was a convenient location downtown.

When Nathan was in Worthington with the Minnesota All-State Lutheran Choir in the summer of 1990, he recalled a story told to him by Debbie Caylor, who had lived in the old depot house. He retold the tale while the wind tossed the water of Lake Okabena into whitecaps and rattled the pages of my tablet. Debbie Caylor Kreigenbring is old now; in fact, she's 98. But she told Nathan of an incident that happened when she was a young girl and lived in the depot-house at the edge of New London.

Her story has to do with faces in a window. She began, "When I was small...oh, let's see, that would be about 1902...when I was about ten, I think...of course I went to bed pretty early. Some little folks nowadays stay up all hours of the night, but not me. I was sent up to my room by 7:30, or maybe 8:00 now an' then. Mine was a second-story room that used to be part of the apartment that the old depot agent lived in.

"Anyway, one night I was about to put out my lamp when something caught my eye. Some motion, maybe. I looked toward the window, and there was a man's face up against the window. I remember it plain as day. Maybe because it scared me so. Maybe 'cause his nose was flat against the window and looked like the biggest part of his face.

"I called my father, but he didn't believe me. It happened a couple more times. Always the same face. But when I told my father, he just said, 'Young lady, I think you have a very active imagination for a ten-year-old. Now try and get to sleep!'

"The day after Thanksgiving that year, my cousin from out in the country came to stay the night. She kept kicking me and I wasn't used to sleeping with anyone, so I woke up in the middle of the night. It was a beautiful, harvest-moon night. I looked out the window to find the man in the moon, and there was that other face again. Same one. I screamed. That woke cousin Edie, and she saw it, too."

He said Nathan went on to say that Jacob, Debbie's father, had a hectic time of it that night. He tried to get everybody settled back down to sleep. He quick pulled down the shade at Debbie's window so she wouldn't see any more reflections, or whatever, in the window. But then he lay awake a long time. It nagged at his mind a bit that Edie had said there really was someone at the window. Edith and Lew's youngest, Edie, was two years older than his own Debbie, and Jacob didn't think she was apt to fib about something like that.

The next morning, Jacob looked around outside before he went to work at the hardware store. He was looking for any impressions that a ladder would have made in the not-yet-frozen ground. There wasn't even any grass broken from a weight bearing down on it. Nor were there any footprints.

"Silly girls!" he burst out. As an afterthought, he checked the window to see how the oiled paper, put there to save fuel, was holding up. Suddenly he saw that a hole about the size of a man's face had been cut into the paper!

From that day on, Jake was a believer.

A month later, when Christmas came around, Debbie rejoiced over the new ice skates her Grandpa and Grandma, visiting from Spicer, had given her. They told her they hoped she would come to Green Lake to try them out the Sunday between the holidays, so they could watch her skate and see how they worked. Debbie said, "I hope I can. And thank you both a lot. I love them. If we can come to your house Sunday, I'll sure bring them along." And she was thinking that would give her a chance to try out her new skates and see Grandpa and Grandma again, too, before vacation ended.

On Sunday, when Jacob was ready to leave for Green Lake, he asked Debbie, "Got your skates?"

Debbie went up to get them from her room. She'd put all her gifts up there after she'd looked at them and handled each one about ten more times. Those skates were the best. None of her friends had figure skates yet. And hers had the sawlike teeth at the toe end, a new development. She could try to do jumps now.

She bent down to pull the skates out from under her bed, and jumped back in surprise. There was a man under her bed! First Debbie thought her brother was teasing her again, but then she remembered he wasn't home. She screamed as she backed out of her room and turned and ran downstairs.

Jacob went up with Debbie "just to check this story out," he said. First he glanced toward the window. Nothing there. He bent down to look under the bed. Nothing unusual there, except the new ice skates. They were sticking halfway out from under the dust ruffle.

Jacob told Debbie, "Forget it! There's no man under your bed. Now, let's get going!"

All the way to Grandpa and Grandma's place near Green Lake, Debbie was frustrated and on the verge of tears. She couldn't explain it. She didn't even know what had happened or how. To her, it was just a fact. She did see a man under her bed. But no one else believed her. She stayed a little closer to her dad that afternoon, and when he wasn't nearby, she sought comfort from Grandma.

That same afternoon, Debbie's older brother George had been out to his Aunt Edith and Uncle Lew's farm, closer to Spicer than to New London. He knew where his father and his sister were, so he decided to walk down there along the railroad tracks. As he stepped rhythmically from one tie to another, he was joined by a man who also walked along smoothly from tie to tie and sometimes balanced very lightly on the rails. They walked and talked for a long time, but to George the time went fast. He was fascinated by the man's tales.

He told George he had been a freight man on that road for "nigh onto thirty years. That was 'fore they made me depot agent. Guess they figgered I was gettin' up in years an' couldn't handle the freight. Tickets? Oh, I could handle them, all right. And that danged telegraph outfit, too. And I didn't have to push the ding-busted turntable around any more, either. Nearly split my guts doin' that when it was a loaded freight car had to be turned around on it."

When George showed up at his grandmother's dining room table just in time for supper, Jacob asked, "Son, why didn't you come to the lake first? Debbie skated just fine, of course," he said with a sly wink, "but you could have saved her a couple tumbles if you'd been there."

George said, "Oh, I was talking to old Mr. Witzke for a while. He was walking along the tracks, too, when I started out from Uncle Lew's. We had quite a talk. He told me --"

Grandma interrupted very quietly, "George, old Mr. Witzke died many years ago. He died at night, in that depot he worked in, in that same room that is Debbie's now."

She asked Debbie to get the maroon-covered photo album with the label "Before 1900" on its front cover. George paged through it until he found old Eby Witzke, labeled "New London's first depot agent." They were look-alikes, for sure, the man on the tracks and the man in the album. George recognized him easily. So did Debbie. His was the face at her window; he was the man under her bed.

After that Christmastime return performance, old Eby Witzke, the first depot agent in New London, was never seen or heard from around there again. And once Debbie understood that it was his spirit that appeared to her, she slept peacefully in his old room.

And now Nathan Swenson sleeps there. When he finishes his homework, he tells Eby goodnight. He thinks of him as a friend. A friendly spirit.

An Orange Ball of Fire?

Henry Schuster's father was Fred Schuster. When Fred was a young man, there weren't any automobiles as there were in Henry's time. When Fred took his sweetheart Matilda out on a date, he drove a one-horse buggy with a top on it. It was an open buggy, so it had no side curtains. It was a one-seater, with no back seat. And no lantern. And in cold weather, you placed a blanket over your legs to keep warm.

Henry told me about a strange experience his father once had. He said, "One evening after Fred took Matilda home in the buggy, he was on his way back to the family farm about five miles away. The horse, a six- or seven-year-old bay called Molly, was well-trained. She had been used on the buggy a lot by all members of the family, so Fred had the opportunity to look around as Molly made her way back to the family farm. Fred might also have dozed off, but suddenly something over to the left caught his attention. He saw something bright. He didn't know what it was. He kept watching and it stayed there, some distance away, off to that side, out there in the field. He stopped the horse. Whatever the thing was, it stopped, too.

"He said it was round. In fact, to him it looked like an orange ball of fire rolling along the ground. But the field didn't catch fire. And he couldn't see any smoke. It couldn't be a reflection of anything on the buggy, as far as he could figure out. And what would it be reflecting in? There weren't any ponds out there. It was just an open, plowed field of black soil. Fred wondered how long this thing would stay with him. He thought, 'No one will ever believe me if I say an orange ball of fire followed me all the way home, but at a distance.'

"He jerked the reins just a little to make Molly hurry a bit more. When she did, the ball of fire moved faster, too. Fred knew there were blinders on the bridle, so he figured Molly wouldn't see the thing and be spooked.

"When Molly reached the lane and turned into the yard, the mysterious ball of fire kept going. It just kept rolling along toward the horizon like a tumbleweed on fire, but it wasn't.

"Fred said later, as he often told the story to his sons, 'I never saw it again, just that one time, and I never figured it out, but I'll tell you one thing - I was mighty glad that thing didn't follow me into the yard.'"

And Henry finished, "There. That's the way my father always told it to me and others. We couldn't figure out what the strange thing was any better than he could, but he said it was true. Maybe *you* can figure it out."

Did More Than Perfume
Rise from the Manure Pile?

Ollie told this story about something that had happened around the turn of the century. Two elderly bachelors had lived on a farm southwest of Worthington and about eleven miles from the Minnesota/Iowa border.

Others in the neighborhood of the farm knew that one day, when the two were out pitching manure, they had a disagreement over something or other. It had led to a big fight - a bad one. So bad, they say, that one of the bachelors killed the other and buried him on the spot, right next to the manure pile.

For nearly four decades after the incident, no matter who lived on the farm, people would see the "dead man" walking across the yard, just as plain as day. Ollie said that his family lived on that farm later on. "When I was sixteen," he said, "me an' my two younger sisters came home once at midnight. When we got into the yard, I looked up and I said, 'There's that man walking across the yard again.' Then I ran in the house and got my 12-gauge shotgun, came out, an' shot the 'man' at close range."

Ollie married, and years later, he often told this story. No matter how many times he told it, his wife never seemed to believe it had really happened. But in 1990 when Ollie told it all to a friend, his wife spoke up, too. She said, "It had to be a ghost. If it had been a real man, he would have been blown to bits. Instead, he just totally disappeared!"

Ollie said, "I never saw the ghost after that. But a few years after we were married, my wife Nellie was bathing the youngsters in the dining room part of the house. We had a tub we could put in there, and it was a little warmer and more private than in the kitchen. I remember it was winter when this happened, and it was getting dark.

"While the kids splashed around, Nell looked out the window toward the other house on our place. She saw a man go across the yard and up to the tenant house, but she thought nothing of it right then. She finished bathing the children and helped them get into their nightshirts. The next day, though, she thought of it again when she was visiting with the lady who lived in the tenant house. Nell said, 'I see you had company last night.'

"Without a bit of hesitation, Hattie answered, 'No, we didn't have company last night.'"

But to this day Nellie is sure she saw a man go into that other house that evening. Or was it the ghost of the man who was buried beside the manure pile?

Problems with the House

When Sandra and Tom Plombon were little more than newlyweds, they were happy to finally find a house in St. Cloud that they could afford to rent. Here they would have more room, too, which they needed since their daughter Sarah had just been born. And here no one would complain about a baby crying for a feeding in the middle of the night, as had happened in an upstairs apartment. Sandra remembers spending a week cleaning the house, but she said she already felt comfortable with the old house as she worked.

About two days after they moved in, Sandra sat in the basement talking with a friend. She remembers telling the friend about the feeling of warmth and security that had come over her. "I really think I'm going to like it here!"

But that feeling didn't last. Baby Sarah wouldn't sleep in her crib at night. She would cry and cry. Singing to her while rocking her helped get her back to sleep, but as soon as she was put down in her crib again, she would cry again.

When Sandra told the doctor they weren't getting any sleep at night because the baby cried all night, he claimed the baby was spoiled. He said to just let her cry. She would get over it. The young mother tried that. She let the baby cry - until Sarah started throwing up. From then on, until they moved out of that house, Sarah slept in her parents' bed. However, later on, after they moved, Sara had no trouble sleeping in her own crib in her own room.

Soon things started affecting Sandra, too. "One night, while I was alone in that same house with Sarah, before we moved out, I suddenly got a strange feeling that something wasn't right. The feeling built up to terror. I grabbed Sarah and held her and sang to her as we sat rocking in a chair in a corner of the dining room. We were still there when Tom came home. I was so scared that night, and I couldn't even offer Tom a reason. I mostly kept the fear to myself.

"Shortly after that, Tom started working nights. Maybe I was just overwrought about nothing, but no way was I going to stay in that house at night *while he was at work.* I started spending those nights at my mother's house. But on a night when we were at home, I went downstairs to the bathroom, which I had done plenty of times before. As I started back toward the door to the stairs, it felt like someone pushed me. I hit the kitchen wall so hard, I was almost knocked out.

"A few days later, I couldn't find Sarah. I searched every room downstairs. Frantic with fear, I ran into the kitchen. There I noticed the door to the upstairs was slightly ajar. I was always careful to close that door because of the stairs. I didn't want Sarah to even try crawling up the steps. I went up to check, and there was Sarah in our bedroom! She couldn't have crawled all the way up. Besides, at eight months, she couldn't have reached the door knob, so how could she have opened the door and then closed it almost all the way behind her?

"Later that spring and into summer, while I was pregnant again, I had serious trouble. As I was walking down the stairs, I felt an impact from behind - more like a force - and I tumbled down the stairs fast. I lost the baby at nine weeks. When I was released from the hospital, I was ready to move. I just wanted to get out of that house.

"While we looked around for a house to buy, I held a 'basement sale' to get rid of some things we didn't need. One customer told me she and her family had lived there at one time. She asked me if we had any problems with the house while we lived there. I didn't realize what she meant at first, so I said, 'Yes, the closet roof leaked and I had to throw some things away.'

"She said, 'No, I mean...' and she looked me in the eye as she spoke almost secretively, '...I mean, did you have any *problems* with the house?'

"Because I still wondered if some of it was all in my mind, and because I didn't know the woman, I said 'No' and didn't tell her any of it. But now I wish I had talked to her more.

"While we were packing, three girls came to see the house. They fell in love with it and were ready to move in anytime. Just a month before we moved out, some force hurled me down the stairs. I didn't ever want to be alone in the house again. I was terrified. I began to wonder if there was an evil presence there, but I didn't tell anyone about it.

"Finally, a week before our moving day, I woke up in the very quiet house. Tom and Sarah were asleep, and everything seemed to be all right, but I couldn't get back to sleep. Suddenly a voice filled the room. It said, 'Sandi' and then a laugh followed. No one else woke up. No one else heard it. But that laugh seemed to go on forever. That night, I knew I couldn't take much more of it. It seemed a long time until morning.

"We moved on schedule. The girls who rented the house next only stayed two months. A lot of people have moved in and out since then. The house was sold twice.

"I still don't have the answer. Most of the ghost stories I've read or heard have been about good spirits, protective ghosts, helpful or kind ghosts. I just wonder, when I think over all those things I felt or experienced, if that house had a jealous or vengeful ghost. I wonder if some woman who lived there earlier maybe lost her child and couldn't stand to see a happy mother and baby. I wonder what that former tenant could have told me about problems she had with the house. I wish I could talk with her again. Maybe I would finally be able to understand what was happening, and why. But I know by now that we don't always have the answers to things that affect us."

A Promise Best Kept

When Mark, his parents, and his three sisters lived in the stucco house in Worthington, it appeared there were others also occupying the house.

One of these non-paying residents would take on the figure of a man in a white lab-type coat over his other clothes. He would be up and about from midnight until around one, walking in the house, checking up on everyone, the way a former doctor might do if he came back to "live" a little longer and continue his professional duties.

Another visitor fit the category of poltergeist. The family often referred to this one as a practical joker. He liked to move things around. That didn't set too well with Mark's father. "He was especially ticked off about one incident," Mark said. "Dad had hung up some brand new lawn chairs in the basement. One day, when he was going fishing, he decided to take the chairs along. He went to get them, but they weren't there. None of us had moved them. A month later, to the very day, the chairs were hanging there again, exactly where they had first been hung. They still had the plastic covering on them.

"The family found other things moved around. Once it was the elf figurines Mom had. Other times, it would be something one of us had put down. For example, if someone laid a wrist watch on the night stand at bedtime, it might be moved to the top of the dresser instead, and sometimes to someplace else in the house, by morning.

"Things didn't always show up right away, but everything 'the joker' took would eventually show up somewhere in the house. Then there was the light in the attic. When we came home at night, we'd notice it was on. By the time we got inside and up there to turn it off, the light would already be off."

Mark said, "It got so we felt like someone else was around all the time. We got used to it. If one of us opened a closet or the attic door, we would feel something...as if someone jumped out at us, like you do when you say 'Boo!' to scare someone.

"Sometimes when my sisters or I were sitting in our rooms doing our homework, we felt that someone else was there watching us, looking over our shoulders. Sometimes I felt a hand resting on my shoulder and I would turn around to see who was there. It never turned out to be one of my family.

"We lived in that house for thirteen years. Later on, I lived in an apartment a couple of blocks away, but I still felt that the poltergeist was there with me. I called it a practical joker. When I confronted it verbally, asking it to return a missing item, that item would be in place again the next morning or, sometimes, in a couple of days. Nothing was ever broken."

Mark related other family experiences, some of them connected with a promise. He said, "While we were living in Kansas, Grandfather made Dad promise never to rent a house, or he would come back to haunt him. Dad thought it a rather strange thing to ask, but he agreed. Soon afterward, he took his family to Worthington where he didn't own a house, so we moved into a rented one near the Worthington Cemetery. That same summer, my great-grandfather died after we had been living in the rented house for just about a week.

"One night I felt someone sitting on the edge of my bed and patting my leg, just like my great-grandfather used to do in real life. I remembered it had always been comforting, but it seemed strange to have it happen now *when he was dead.* I woke up wide and Great-grandfather said, 'Don't worry. Everything will be all right. I won't be seeing you this summer when you come back to Kansas to visit, but I'll always be nearby watching over you.' Then he disappeared, and I realized his spirit had visited me.

"I was awake, so I went downstairs to get something to drink. When I walked by my parents' bedroom, I looked that way to see if they were awake. There was my grandfather, standing at the end of their bed. He had a scowl on his face and he was shaking his finger at my dad and saying, 'I told you so!' He had come back to my dad the same night my great-grandfather had come back to me. The difference was that I was comforted and encouraged by great-grandfather's visit. But my dad felt threatened and scolded by grandfather's return.

"My parents both saw him there. They talked about it and decided it was time to buy a house, *or we would keep getting visits from the departed.* That was when my dad first told me about the promise his father had made him agree to, and that was when I started believing in ghosts.

"I still wake up sometimes to find my great-grandfather appearing and telling me, 'Just hang in there and everything will be all right.' Then he helps me relax and get to sleep the way he used to do.

"As for Dad, he realized that the promise he had made

to his father was one that had better be kept, and he never moved his family into a rented house again."

A Prophetic Passenger

About ten years have passed since Nettie told this story at a Bible study class. Nettie told the group, "You know my daughter is attending Mankato State. A few weeks ago, she and two other girls were coming home to Worthington for the weekend.

"Kim, who was driving, made it a practice not to pick up a hitchhiker. This time, though, she did because the man was wearing a suit - and looked exceptionally neat. The girls were all riding in front, so he got in back. Everyone felt a little awkward at first, and no one said anything. It was pretty quiet in the car. But then, as they drove along, the back-seat passenger said, 'Jesus is coming soon.'

"The girls didn't know what to say, so they just sat there and Kim kept on driving.

"A little while later, one of the girls thought of something she could say to him. She turned to speak, but there was no one there. They hadn't stopped the car or slowed down noticeably or anything. They couldn't figure out how he got out. Kim drove on until they got to a country gas station along the way. All three were shaken by what had happened, and they were ready to stop and tell someone about it.

"They told their story to the attendant, hoping he could help them make sense out of it. When they had finished, he said, 'You are the seventeenth car that has stopped and told me that same story.'"

Much later, Nettie told the story a second time to another group gathered for a Bible study. She finished with, "You know, when I told this story the first time, no one said anything for a while. Now I'm asking you, what do you make of it?"

After some thought, Louise ventured, "Well...if he didn't actually get out, but he wasn't there any more when she turned around..."

Henrietta interrupted. "He must have been a spirit! We've just been talking about spirits and good angels and things like that..."

"Yes," Nettie said, "and that's exactly what I've been thinking. He - or whatever, whoever - must have been one of God's guardian angels, keeping watch over the girls."

"Keeping watch over them and sixteen other cars full of people traveling home," Louise continued. "And that's the only explanation there could be! How else could he get in and out of all those cars? Isn't that something!"

Others who had heard about or experienced something similar shared their stories. In each case, the hitchhiker was wearing a suit and gave a message of comfort or hope before he disappeared mysteriously from the moving vehicle. To be sure, the Bible study for that day continued at a more animated pace than it had been or would be for quite some time.

Who Held the Warning Light?

This first of Annie Meyers' stories happened many, many years ago. Annie doesn't remember it happening; she was just a girl then. But she heard her mother tell it often enough to remember it, and she doesn't mind repeating it.

Annie said that Dr. C. C. May, the physician who had come to Adrian in 1886 to start his practice, was called out of town one rainy night. "That would have been in the early 1900s," she said. Dr. May couldn't just jump into his car and turn on the ignition. He didn't have a car. He took his bag and left by horse and buggy to go to the farm where he was needed.

Just before he reached the wooden bridge on the outskirts of Adrian, he saw a light. He knew it wasn't an approaching buggy light because it didn't keep coming closer. Instead, it seemed to be swinging back and forth from one side of the road to the other, and it kept on swinging.

The doctor called out, but no one answered. Dr. May, knowing time was important in sickness, would have gone on, but his horse stopped. It wouldn't budge, not even with coaxing. The doctor had to get on his way. He thought of throwing his coat over the horse's head and moving forward, but instead he turned the spooked horse and the buggy around and went to the farm by another road. When he had taken care of the patient, he went on back to his home in Adrian, again by a different route from the usual one.

The next day, everyone in town was talking about how the rainstorm had flooded the creek and how the "raging

Kanaranzi" had completely washed out the wooden bridge at the edge of Adrian the evening before.

When Doctor May heard the news, he realized his life had been saved by that warning light. Perhaps not only *his* life - many of the people of the community depended on him as their doctor. If he had ignored the light...if he had tried to cover his horse's head and lead him across...he shuddered to think of what his fate might have been.

And ever since that night, though a new cement bridge has replaced the old one, Annie says the young people of Adrian never hang around it long. They say they have an eerie feeling when they go down there. The swimming hole below the new bridge might be as good as it ever was, but somehow they never feel at ease, even in the daytime. They keep thinking of that warning light and they wonder how it got there, who swung it.

A Spirit Stronger Than Nails

When Annie Meyers was very young, her Grandpa and Grandma Schumans lived in Adrian. Their neighbors had strange things happening in their house, especially in the room upstairs on the west side. Annie remembers her grandparents telling about what happened there.

The neighbor lady liked a neat house, they said, but she complained that no matter how hard she tried, she could never keep that one room straightened up. One of the most exasperating circumstances was that when she adjusted the shades and fluffed the curtains, they were never left that way. In fact, they'd be pulled down. The couple even went so far as to nail the shades and curtains to the window frames, but would invariably find them ripped off and piled on the floor. The clothes in the dresser drawers in that room were also rearranged frequently, sometimes pulled entirely out of the drawers and scattered around the room. That was pretty exasperating, but the couple didn't want to give up. Eventually they left, and the house was moved off that lot. Apparently the spirit was stronger than nails and stronger than the couple's courage in the matter.

A Letter Edged in Black

Annie Meyers' grandfather and grandmother Durban stayed in Switzerland when other members of the family left for America. Among those who crossed the ocean were Annie's father Anton, his brother Sebastian, and their sister Magdalene. Before he married, Anton lived near Dubuque, Iowa where he worked for a farmer and lived with the farmer's family.

One night between 12:30 and 1:00, Anton woke up because it felt like something was poking him in the ribs. He sat up, and there stood his father before him. He saw him plain as could be, long beard and all. His father called him by name. In a firm, yet gentle tone, he said, "Anton."

At that time, Uncle Sebastian was single and working for a farmer near Adrian. Sebastian also had a brief visit from his father that night, but he crawled under the covers and didn't get out until morning.

Their sister Magdalene, who lived on a small farm southwest of Adrian, saw their father too, that same night. But she knew this couldn't be. He lived in Switzerland and couldn't just suddenly appear in Minnesota. She knew that even the mail from Europe, coming by ship, took a few weeks to cross the Atlantic.

About a month after the appearances of their father, the family members all received a letter edged in black. It informed them that their father had died between 12:30 and 1:00 on the same night that he had appeared to three of his children in Iowa and Minnesota. In America.

Swamp Ghosts

When Henry was a young boy, he lived with his family in Murray County in southwest Minnesota. He remembers that there was a lot of wetland around there, on and near his father's farm.

Most folks knew about Lake Shetek and four other neighboring lakes that all together covered almost 4,000 acres with water. There were good fishing areas. There were swampy areas, too; one was Slaughter Slough, where white settlers had been attacked in 1862. The outlet dam on the area's largest lake formed the headwaters basin of the Des Moines River, so Murray County had a lot of wetland, but good farmland, too.

The old-timers had a lot of stories, some related to historical events, some reminiscences about things that happened in everyday life. Young boys and girls heard the stories from their elders in the long hours when the weather forced people indoors, or prevented trips to town or to the neighbors'. And sometimes the youngsters lay awake wondering about the stories. Were they real? Would they ever see a trapper and his wooden oxcart, or an Indian, or a ghost? They heard such stories often enough to make them wonder.

Henry says that he and his friend Herman used to go out exploring the timber and the prairie around their fathers' farms. The twelve-year-olds stalked the woods for wild animals, sometimes pretending they had flushed out a lazy bear or a mountain lion. They searched the tall grasses of the prairie areas until they lost each other trying to find the tallest Big Bluestem, even though it was much taller than their five-foot heights.

Sometimes the boys kicked around in the leaves between the trees and the shore of the lake. Once they had activated the snakes that lay in sunny spots on warm fall days, they could chase them back into their holes. Then they could follow the wild mink along the rocky banks and watch them duck under the lake's surface among the reeds.

One Saturday, their outing started later than usual. First they had to go to confirmation class at their rural church. When Henry's father came to pick them up, he stayed a while to visit with the pastor. Once home, they had to finish their lunch before they could go exploring. Then Herman had to gather the eggs because he hadn't gotten up early enough to do it after breakfast. When they finally met at the edge of the slough nearest their farms, it was the middle of the afternoon.

As they waded through the tall grasses, Henry wondered why his father didn't harvest the side oats brome or the turkeyfoot grass.

A little later, Herman found some bottle gentian growing in a low spot. "Come back a minute, Henry," Herman called to his fellow-explorer. "Here in the ditch, something broke off the stems of some bottle gentians. Look at the "bottles" on the stems. They're blue, and they're closed so tight that you can't even see the pollen inside. I wonder who broke them off."

"Oh, probably just some deer that laid around here last night," Henry responded. "They have to rest somewhere, and they couldn't see the wildflowers in the night."

"Or care if they did lay on 'em. Let's go on over there, closer to the slough," Herman suggested.

"Okay, but it's going to start getting dark soon and we have to get back home before it does. I promised."

"I know, Henry. So did I. We probably shouldn't have trailed that mink so long. But it was fun to watch it. It looked like a long, skinny cat with a long, fluffy tail. It was sure different from the ugly, bare tail of a possum or a rat."

"That's for sure. It must have its house in among those reeds somewhere near where we lost it."

"I'm going to look for that old wreck of a boat we found last year on the edge of the slough. I think the water's low enough this year that we can climb into it and watch the ducks from there."

"I'm going the other way and look for that old oak tree. It's farther away from the slough, but not all that far. Hermie, when you find the boat, give a whistle and I'll answer you back from wherever I am. When I find the tree, I'll climb up and sit in it and see if I can see the boat from there. Those branches are just like benches, only they're all twisted up around each other. See you from there!"

About a half hour passed before Henry heard Herman's whistle. He whistled back as he climbed one branch higher. He looked toward where the boat should be, but it was nearly dusk and not as easy to be sure what he was seeing. Besides, his eyes were playing tricks on him. What was going on? Was there someone out there on the slough, lighting candles or hay twists? What he saw looked like blinking stars that were strung out over the slough, and the slough was lighting up as if the night sky and the swamp had traded places. He had always been near the slough at daylight. What made it so different when evening came on?

Herman wondered why he couldn't see Henry up in the tree. But then it was a ways away from the boat, and it was almost dark now. He was about to whistle three times, a signal that they'd better meet at the old raft they tried to build once, when he heard a loon out on the lake. Glancing toward Lake Shetek, he saw a lot of little lights, like flames flickering, dancing around just above the earth. Not over on the lake, but between him and the lake, over the swampy places around the wettest part of the slough. He wondered what was out there. The darker it got, the brighter the little flames were and the more dancing lights he could see. It was weird.

Herman got out of the boat and gave one triple-whistle signal and listened for the answer. Hearing it, he started toward the ruins of the raft. He thought, "It's a good thing we've been out here a lot, or it would be easy to get lost, and it's really time to be going home."

Henry slid and swung from one branch to another until he, too, was on the ground and on his way toward the old raft. He was reluctant to go home. He wished he could stay and watch the lights and see if they showed all night long. And what if...

But then he was at the raft and saw that Herman had gotten there first. Oh, well, another time he'd beat Herman to it.

All the way home they compared notes. The main conversation was the dancing flames. With the land so wet around there, how could there be fire, or even little flames that died out as soon as they lit up? Herman remembered that his grandmother had a plant once, by the fence in her yard, that she called a "gas plant." It had tall stems with little pinkish-lavender flowers when it bloomed. The flowers were all along the stems, and when grandpa went out in the yard in the evenings with him, he'd let Herman hold a lighted match near the bottom of the stalk and watch the little flames light up from the bottom to the top of the plant. Whoosh, it went fast, he remembered. The whole thing only lasted a few seconds. But there weren't any of those plants out here in the swamp. They had never seen anything except the grasses and the wildflowers like the bottle gentians and New England asters.

Henry mentioned the Indian mound that had been farmed over for a long time. That made him think of the Indians that used to live there and the white settlers killed not very far away. In fact, their teacher said that happened right at that slough and that's why it was named Slaughter Slough.

Herman shivered. He said, "I wish you hadn't thought of that. My brother always teases me. When I get a little scared he always says, 'Maybe it was a ghost.' Do you think there might be ghosts of those early people hanging around? Do you think they might have been trying to scare us tonight? The preacher was saying something this morning about good and evil spirits."

"Well, we never saw this happen before. But then, we never were out here at night before. We sure never would see the lights in the daytime. Why would they come out at night, though? What do you think the lights are?"

Now Herman tried his brother's tactics. "...maybe ghosts?"

The two started for home. They ran as fast as they

could. Neither cared who beat who this time. They grabbed each other's hand and ran side by side until they could see their houses, across the road from each other, and the lights in the windows. It would be a long time before they explored anywhere near Slaughter Slough late in the day.

Time Smiles the While

Lucille and Bob had room for antiques in their home on Nobles Street in Worthington. Lucille was very much into antiques and collectibles, and her family and relatives knew and respected that. In fact, a niece of hers once came all the way from Oklahoma to get a hurricane lamp she had been wanting.

Lucille and her niece brought the lamp down from the attic. It was an old, ornate piece. The niece thought once she got the lamp home and assembled, the globes would be very pretty, lighted in the evenings.

Lucille said, "Each part of this lamp is important because of its unusual size, so we must be sure to pack all the parts."

As they visited, Lucille wrapped each part of the lamp separately and put plenty of packing around the two globes. Before she sealed the box, she thought through the parts one by one.

"Did we wrap the small part that the lower globe rests on?" she asked her niece.

"You mean the part where the switch is? I saw that in one of the bundles you wrapped."

"No, I mean the fitting that has three arms. The bottom globe has to sit on it to stay in place when the whole thing goes together again. Without that, it won't be much of a lamp. We'd better look for it."

They went through all the bundles again. They checked the corners of the big corrugated box and felt under the piles of packing paper on the floor. Lucille went up to the attic to make sure the part hadn't been left up there. It wasn't anywhere in sight.

The niece needed to get on her way again, so she prepared to leave without that one part. "It's got to be here somewhere. I'll send it as soon as I find it," Lucille assured her. "I'm just sorry you won't be able to put the lamp together as soon as you get home."

That lamp was only one of many interesting furnishings and collectibles in their home. Bob and Lucille also had an attractive clock their son had brought back from Germany. They were used to it being there on the wall. Bob was the keeper of the key.

Lucille said, "I never fooled with the clock. I was always afraid I'd wind it too tight or something, so I was glad Bob took care of it.

"It wasn't one of those you had to pull weights on. He wound it with a key. When he finished, he always dropped the key into the space below where the pendulum swings. That way it was always handy when he needed it. And it was easy to find, because the space was pretty roomy. The whole clock was about three feet tall and a foot wide."

The next time the clock needed to be wound after their niece left, Bob found the key in its usual place. He also found the missing part of the lamp. It wasn't wrapped. It was simply hiding inside the bottom of the clock. No one knew how it got there. Lucille knows for sure that she wouldn't have put it there, because she never opened the clock. And Bob wasn't home when the lamp was brought down from the attic for wrapping and packing.

How the part of the lamp got placed in the clock will always be a question. Unless, of course, the clock knows and tells, in time.

"Spirit Little Cedar"

On March 25, 1991 the *Cook County News-Herald* featured a photograph of The Witch Tree, an ancient living pine growing on the rocks near Grand Portage.

According to the cutline, students in Layne Kennedy's winter photography class had spent a morning at the site. The photo showed them dressed for the weather, standing in what looked like snow, with chunky ice slabs surrounding the huge rocks supporting the tree.

The tree, popular with artists and photographers, has character. Growing between huge rocks in the water, its trunk is gnarled and twisted as though it had danced in the wind even as it grew. Near the top of the braided trunk, branches appear to unwind. They continue to spiral somewhat as they support a sparse top growth that makes up only about a third of the tree's height.

Those who view the tree have varied reactions. Some remark about the twisted, almost knotted trunk. Others notice the limited top growth, some branch ends almost stripped naked by winds and ice storms. An artist or a photographer might see something in the silhouette the tree makes against the lake, or in the line and direction of movement in the trunk and branches. Some may admire the tree's perseverance - seeming to grow from rock, battling the weather on the rock-bound shore, yet surviving.

The Chippewa, long-time inhabitants of the area, have another name for the tree. They call it "Spirit Little Cedar" and they hold it in reverence. When they prepare to cross over that part of Lake Superior by birch bark canoe to Isle Royale, they first make tobacco offerings to their "Spirit

Little Cedar," asking it to calm the lake for them.

Shawn Perich, former editor of the *Cook County News-Herald*, said the Voyageurs of long ago also made the tobacco offerings, asking for fair winds.

It was the artist Dewey Albinson who later coined the name, "Witch Tree."

Those familiar with the area suggest that if you travel to Cook County and go on to Grand Portage's Witch Tree at Hat Point on Lake Superior, you should not fear the spirit that lives on in the tree, or be afraid that a witch will bring you harm. Rather, remember how many generations of Chippewas have respected and revered their "Spirit Little Cedar," making tobacco offerings in exchange for safe journeys on the waters.

Those generations of Chippewas included fathers and grandfathers who heard the Great Spirit's voice as they fished and hunted for game. Legend has it that they asked for protection from wrathful winds and turbulent waves. Offerings were also made by the generations of Chippewas who gathered the abundant wild rice, and by young lovers crossing the lake to rendezvous.

Others looked up to their "Spirit Little Cedar" as they crossed the waters of Lake Superior: young men going to meet in their soldiers' lodge, old men gathering around council fires, and the braves going off to confront enemy Sioux. Indian women, bidding a final farewell to their papooses lost forever during the fierce winters, made their offerings as they trudged along the shore or canoed to the burial places of their people.

To the Chippewa, the tree symbolized a good spirit, one to be respected rather than feared.

A Wizened Face

When his two sons were attending Mankato State, Worthington Attorney Cy Bernardy bought a house in Mankato. The old, three-story structure on Warren Street provided living quarters for his sons as well as rooms to rent to others.

The house was neither unusual nor fancy, but it was adequate. The first time the family went through it, they found one strange thing in the attic, a huge vat. It was about the only thing up there. The only use Cy could imagine for it seemed logical for an old house: a water-storage tank on the highest level would supply adequate water pressure to the bathroom on the second floor. The vat was no longer used, since the bathrooms had modern plumbing, but it was still up there.

In August of 1980, Cy's sons Chuck and Chris moved into the house, along with a few others who rented rooms there.

Students would ask each other, "As I walk through the house, I get the impression someone is following me. But when I stop and turn around, there's never anyone there. Does that happen to you, too?" They found that they all had had that experience, and each vowed he wasn't guilty of following the others.

During the night, the occupants often heard someone or something pounding, making a terrible racket. "It had to be someone or something striking that vat in the attic. None of us would do that," Cy's son said. "And there aren't any radiators or steam pipes. The house is heated by forced air."

As the year passed, the students found that the noises were heard year 'round. Chuck, Cy's older son, lived in an east bedroom. Eventually they learned that a man had committed suicide in that room. The students reported that they always felt the presence and heard the banging. They wondered if those incidents had anything to do with the man's death.

For a while, a young lady with the same last name as the dead man's lived in the house. While she did, there was no "presence", no strange feeling, no terrible racket. While everyone noticed it was gone, no one could explain it.

When Chuck graduated and moved out, another young man who came to Mankato to attend college took over his room. This new occupant knew about the suicide, but it didn't bother him until one night when he woke up to see a face in his room. He described it to Chris this way: "I saw greenish eyes set in a wizened face and framed in white hair. But there was no one there."

Chris said, "Let's find out what that man who killed himself looked like." The next morning, the two young men crossed the empty lot next door and knocked on a neighbor's door. They asked the woman living there if she knew the man who used to live in their house and what he looked like. The neighbor described to a wrinkle the face the student had seen in the night.

Cy kept the house for a few years after his sons had both finished college there in Mankato. The young man who had lived in Chuck's old room managed the house while he attended school. His girl friend moved into the bedroom Chris had used. One night when she was studying, the lights went out. Trying to figure out why, she looked up. What she saw then was a pair of eyes very much like the eyes of the dead man the neighbor lady had described earlier. It scared the girl so thoroughly that she never went upstairs alone in that house again.

One night not long after that incident, the manager heard the banging again. At that time, Chris was insulating the attic with six- to eight-inch thick fiberglass. When he had finished his work, he picked up his tools and left the attic, making sure that all the windows were securely fastened. Other than the old vat, there was nothing up there.

Nevertheless, as the manager checked the attic for the source of the latest racket, he saw a dark object lying on the floor beneath the loose window that was banging against its frame. When he went to pick it up, he found it was an old, leather-bound diary. He read a few entries, but felt that he was intruding in someone else's personal, private thoughts. He replaced the diary on the floor beneath the window, closed and latched it, and went downstairs.

After Cy had sold the house, the manager remarked, "I'll always wonder if that diary belonged to the dead man. Was it there all the while? Or was that window opened one more time to return the diary to its home? Did the spirit of the man who died there leave the diary as his final farewell? What would the entries have revealed, if I had been brave enough to read more of them? Do you suppose the diary is still up there?"

A Game We Play

It had to be haunted. There was no other explanation.

It seemed strange to Jerry and Andrea that before they moved into their house in 1975 as newlyweds, no other family had lived there for more than two years.

Worse yet, the people they bought the property from had only lived there about ten months. Researching the abstract, they found that seven or eight families had lived there within the last ten years. Why? It was twenty acres of gently rolling hills with mature pine trees and abundant wildlife.

Andrea couldn't keep still and wonder about it any longer. With a giggle she said, "Maybe it's haunted!" But she was thinking, "Well, what else?"

"Maybe we should start researching the obituaries," said Andrea.

"Are you serious?"

"Well, if there isn't something weird here that scared them away, why would they all go through the work of moving in and then out again so soon? The only family that seemed to care bought the place from the sister who had inherited it. No one else did much in the way of improvement after that."

Jerry passed it off as a bit unusual, but nothing more.

Andrea wasn't sure. They had been married only a short time when they moved into this house in Isanti County. She'd hoped they could be happy there. She'd intended to stay. But...

One bright sunny Saturday afternoon in late May, Andrea would much rather have been outside, but instead she was vacuuming the floors. Above the din of the machine, she thought she heard water running. She also thought she was alone in the house. Jerry was supposed to be outside, and sure enough, when she looked out, he was walking into the barn.

"I shut off the vacuum," Andrea said. The sound of water running seemed to be coming from the bathroom. "I cautiously sneaked up the two steps (not knowing why I was sneaking), turned the corner, and found that both faucets in the sink were turned on, running full blast."

From that day on and over a period of about ten months, there were more strange unexplained occurrences.

"Almost a month after that first surprise," Andrea said, "I took a day off. I planned to finish organizing my first real kitchen. Suddenly a rumbling, roaring sound drowned out my thoughts. It was quite frightening, especially since I couldn't identify it.

"I went to check the basement. I opened the door, holding my breath. A wave of hot air immediately engulfed me. I thought the house was on fire. Slamming the door shut, I started for the phone, wondering who to call, wondering what our fire number was.

"I calmed down a little, and opened the door again. There was no fire. It was just heat, no smoke. The furnace was running! That's what the rumbling, roaring sound was.

"But why? It was June! The thermostat on the wall was set at 52°, as low as it could go. And it was 74° outside, so why did the furnace come on?

"I didn't know what else to do, so I called the fuel oil company. Fifteen minutes later, the service man's only conclusion was that I should unscrew the fuse. The problem never happened again.

"A few weeks later, I was having a cup of coffee in my kitchen. It was a thoroughly enjoyable, still summer morning. But not for long. A loud crash boomed through the silence.

"Splashing coffee all over, I dashed upstairs to see what was going on. A window had slammed shut. Not just any window. It was the one I couldn't get open a month earlier. When I finally did, I left it open, until one rainy day when I had to fight with it to get it shut again."

It seemed to her that a pattern was developing: the next incident occurred a month later.

"Our black lab puppy had crept up into our big old overstuffed chair. He knew he wasn't supposed to be on the furniture, but he wanted a soft place to sleep.

"From the kitchen, where I was washing dishes, I saw him there. I said, 'Hey Gus, you'd better get your little bones out of that chair! You know you can't be on the furniture!' I had turned my back to dry my hands when I heard a sudden yelp and a heavy thud. I rushed into the living room. There was Gus, splayed out on the floor in front of the chair. He was awake now, and the look on his innocent little face was one of pure astonishment. I wondered how he could have fallen out of the chair when he was snuggled way back in it, sound asleep."

She had a hard time convincing anyone that these things really had happened, until Jerry also experienced some peculiar occurrences. Not long after the dog incident, they were both in the house briefly one evening after supper. It was one of those hot, still August nights, muggy and threatening to storm.

"Suddenly we heard a bang and a shattering of glass. I wondered if someone had shot out a window or thrown something through one. We ran to the second-story bedroom to find that the window had shattered. The window frame had fallen into the room, and the glass splinters were everywhere."

They looked at each other in amazement and checked everywhere for clues. The puzzle had no solution. Where had the force come from that caused the window to burst inward?

"I think that was when my husband began to believe my theory about a spirit being in the house."

The next incident impressed Jerry. They had just come home from work and were standing on opposite sides of the living room, looking through their mail. Suddenly, the large window fan on the floor near the kitchen doorway came on.

Without looking up, Andrea said, "Jerry, we don't need the fan on right now, do we? It's 68°."

"I know." he said, engrossed in a letter. "Why did you turn it on?"

"I didn't. You did. Didn't you?"

"No, I didn't..."

They turned simultaneously to look at the fan whirring away at top speed, eight feet away from each of them, although neither of them had flipped the switch.

"That winter the clincher came," Andrea reported. "I had heard a tapping in the hallway the night before, but I didn't mention it. I thought my husband, the skeptic, might reserve a room for me somewhere and call an attendant to come with one of those long-sleeved jackets to escort me out.

"But when I heard the tapping the second night, I woke Jerry. I quietly said his name and shook him.

"'What? What's the matter?' he burst out.

"I whispered, 'Shh! Listen!'

"He listened. He said, 'What's that tapping?'

"Bingo! A True Believer!" Andrea thought.

They both thought out all the possible causes of the tapping. Icicles dripping? Maybe. But it was ten below zero and nothing could have been melting. A squirrel? A mouse or a bat? No, the tapping was too rhythmical. It was more like a metronome. But where? How?

It had to be a ghost.

They decided to do some research. They wanted to find out who the spirit was, where it came from, why it revealed itself to them.

"We contacted some of the oldtimers in the neighborhood. One explanation came to us when we found out about the root cellar. It had been just outside our family room door. The same man who had built the main part of our house in 1950 had built the root cellar. Little good it did him, though."

Local legend had it that this man, a bachelor whom we'll call Jonathan, was terrified of thunderstorms. During a severe storm in 1953, Jonathan fled to his root cellar; but in the strong wind a large pine tree fell directly on top of the cellar. It cracked the slabs that formed the roof and ceiling in two! Both halves fell into the root cellar.

"After the storm, a neighbor went to check on Jonathan, as is the custom in the country. He found Jonathan, backed up against the wall, dead. Since there were no serious injuries, it was assumed that he died of fright. Right there in what is now our back yard."

They later learned about another possible origin of their ghost. In the early 60s, one occupant who lived there with his wife and children had developed high blood pressure. The medications of the time helped, but they had a serious side-effect: deep depression. As this man we'll call Tom continued to take his medication, he became more and more depressed. His wife Edna and the kids were beginning to worry.

One afternoon, Andrea said, Edna and the boys went to town for groceries. When they returned an hour or so later, Tom wasn't in the house. They looked around outside and called his name, but he didn't respond.

Edna suspected something might be terribly wrong. She took the children into the house before she called a neighbor to come and help her look for Tom.

Andrea continued, "The neighbor came right over and continued the search. He found Tom in the barn, dead. He had hanged himself.

"We have had no serious problems with the house recently. No furnace or fans running on their own. After seventeen years, we are still here and we still love our place. It's just once in a while now that we hear an odd sound or feel that something is different. When the kids ask about it, I just smile and say, 'Oh, it's just our ghost, checking up on us.' But he doesn't come around often.

"That might be because I finally confronted the ghost the last time he made his presence known. I got up enough nerve to say 'Now look. We aren't going to get scared and run. We love it here and we plan to stay. Don't you worry, we'll take good care of your place for you and for us, since it's our now. So you can just leave. Please go, and be at peace!'

And now Andrea and Jerry's kids have a new game they play. If they hear a tapping - and it's a little tap these days - they tap back. But sometimes they discover it's one of their parents in the next room, playing their game with them.

Andrea concluded, "I wonder how things will go for the next family to occupy this house, when Jerry and I are ancient and can no longer enjoy it and take care of it...will Jonathan or Tom come around again to check up on the new owners?"

About the author:

Ruth D. Hein grew up in Van Horne, Iowa, as the middle child in a ghost-free Lutheran parsonage. With an M.A. from the University of Northern Iowa, she taught high school English and creative writing for 28 years, 21 of those in Decorah. Ruth now lives with her husband, Ken, on a small acreage near Worthington, Minnesota, where she collects ghost stories and wrote the historical column for the Worthington *Daily Globe* for 14 years.